Transnational Political Islam

Critical Studies on Islam

Series Editors: Azza Karam (Programme Director at the World Conference of Religions for Peace, New York) and Ziauddin Sardar (Editor of the critical international journal of contemporary art and culture, *Third Text*)

The Road to Al-Qaeda
The Story of Bin Laden's Right-hand Man
Montasser al-Zayyat

Islam in the Digital Age
E-Jihad, Online Fatwas and Cyber Islamic Environments
Gary R. Bunt

Iraqi Invasion of Kuwait
Religion, Identity and Otherness in the Analysis of War and Conflict
Hamdi A. Hassan

Islam and Modernity
Muslims in Europe and the United States
Iftikhar H. Malik

Hizbu'llah
Politics and Religion
Amal Saad-Ghorayeb

Transnational Political Islam

Religion, Ideology and Power

Edited by
Azza Karam

Foreword by
John Esposito

PLUTO PRESS

First published 2004 by Pluto Press
345 Archway Road, London N6 5AA

www.plutobooks.com

British Library Cataloguing in Publication Data
A catalogue record for this book is available from the British Library

ISBN 0 7453 1626 3 hardback
ISBN 0 7453 1625 5 paperback

Library of Congress Cataloging in Publication Data
Transnational political Islam : religion, ideology and power / edited by
Azza Karam.
        p. cm. — (Critical studies on Islam)
Includes bibliographical references.
    ISBN 0–7453–1626–3 — ISBN 0–7453–1625–5 (pbk.)
    1. Islam and politics. 2. Globalization—Political aspects. 3. Power (Social
sciences) 4. Ideology. I. Karam, Azza M. II. Series.
    JC49.T73 2003
    320.5'5'0917671—dc21

                                                            2003009942

10   9   8   7   6   5   4   3   2   1

Designed and produced for Pluto Press by
Chase Publishing Services, Fortescue, Sidmouth EX10 9QG, England
Typeset from disk by Stanford DTP Services, Northampton, England

In memory of my mother, Rokayya Nafei,
and in gratitude to Mia Berden.

Contents

Critical Studies on Islam

Series Editors: Azza Karam and Ziauddin Sardar

Islam is a complex, ambiguous term. Conventionally it has been used to describe religion, history, culture, civilisation and worldview of Muslims. But it is also impregnated with stereotypes and post-modern notions of identity and boundaries. The diversity of Muslim peoples, cultures, and interpretations, with their baggage of colonial history and postcolonial present, has transformed Islam into a powerful global force.

This unique series presents a far-reaching, critical perspective on Islam. It analyses the diversity and complexity of Islam through the eyes of people who live by it. Provocative and thoughtful works by established as well as younger scholars will examine Islamic movements, the multilayered questions of Muslim identity, the transnational trends of political Islam, the spectre of ethnic conflict, the political economy of Muslim societies and the impact of Islam and Muslims on the West.

The series is built around two fundamental questions. How are Muslims living, thinking and breathing Islam? And how are they rethinking and reformulating it and shaping and reshaping the global agendas and discourses?

As Critical Studies on Islam seeks to bridge the gap between academia and decision-making environments, it will be of particular value to policy-makers, politicians, journalists and activists, as well as academics.

Dr Azza Karam is a Program Director at the World Conference of Religions for Peace (WCRP) International Secretariat based in New York. She has worked as a consultant and trainer with the United Nations and various Middle Eastern and European NGOs, and has lectured and published extensively on conflict, Islam, the Middle East and the politics of development issues. Her books include *Women, Islamisms and State: Contemporary Feminisms in Egypt* (1998), *A Woman's Place: Religious Women as Public Actors* (ed.) (2002) and *Women in War and Peace Building* (forthcoming).

Ziauddin Sardar is a well-known writer, broadcaster and cultural critic. He is the editor of the critical international journal of contemporary art and culture *Third Text* and considered a pioneering writer on Islam. He is the author of several books for Pluto Press, most recently *Islam, Postmodernism and Other Futures: A Ziauddin Sardar Reader,* edited by Sohail Inayatullah and Gail Boxwell.

Acknowledgements

The idea for this book first emerged in the latter part of 1996, after the conclusion of my earlier studies on Islamism in the context of a PhD at the University of Amsterdam, and in the midst of an engaging conversation with Pluto's managing director, Roger van Zwanenburg. It was clear to me then, and certainly globally affirmed today, that political Islam was a force to be reckoned with and one that would be with us, in various guises, for some time to come. Not only did Roger agree to consider this book for publication, but he also agreed to engage Dr Ziauddin Sardar (one of my mentors) and me as series editors for Pluto's Critical Studies on Islam series, in which this book features. Roger must be acknowledged for his vision and constant advice.

Having moved from one continent to another, it became increasingly difficult to follow up the authors and for me to be duly diligent in responding to their insightful essays for this book. I am therefore most grateful for the patience of the various contributors – Amr Hamzawy, Fred Abrahams, Jan Hjärpe, Jan Nederveen Pieterse and Valérie Amiraux – who have been kind enough to stick around despite my silences, and to respond to my erratic – and often frantic – communications. Not only is this their book, but they have taught me a lot. I am also indebted to John Esposito for being an inspiration through his own work and a supportive colleague during this process.

I am grateful for comments on earlier drafts – and much discussion – from Dr P.L. de Silva and Dr Mostafa Karam, both of whom would not let me forget my obligation to complete this work. Their encouragement is priceless. My boss (and colleague), Dr William Vendley, continues to benefit me with his insights on the unique peace-making role of religion and on US foreign policy. Bob Smiley, former director of the Presbyterian UN office, has been a wonderful sounding board and a valuable source of information and references when the cross-Atlantic moves left me looking frantically for my books and articles. My friends and colleagues, Judith Hertz, Kyoichi Sugino, Jennifer Butler, Jeffery Huffines, Jihan AbuZeid, Mahmoud Gebriel and Fatma Hassan, have all been invaluable as ongoing pillars of support, especially when combining a working day of over ten hours with the time to complete this book was about to make me give up the whole enterprise. I owe Ayesha Hasan a huge debt of gratitude for helping me input my editorial comments and changes, and especially for her assistance on the references and bibliography. I also want to thank Lisa Stuffle for her patience and technical assistance with an awesome aspect of technology: the computer. And special thanks to the copy editor, Ruth Willats, for her patience and thorough editing,

For their trust in me and for their prayers, I wish to thank my late mother, Rokayya Nafei, my father and brother, Mostafa and Mohammed Karam, and my in-laws, Cedric de Silva and Melodie de Silva. I also wish to convey my sincerest thanks and admiration to Mia Berden for making the enterprise of study and writing a possibility many years ago, and for continuing to inspire me with her faith and wisdom.

Several forums have been important benchmarks here: in October 2002, the Cincinnati Council of World Affairs symposium on the Clash of Civilizations; the Carnegie Council for International Affairs roundtable on religion and peacemaking; and West Point Academy Terrorism Course. I am grateful to all the panellists, participants and students for their questions and stimulating discussions. The Committee of Religious NGOs at the United Nations warrants a bow here for enabling me to benefit from the many presentations I was invited to make on political Islam, in which various NGO activists, UN officials and academics responded, guided and critiqued the thought process that went into this book. For all those I may not have mentioned, thank you.

Foreword

John Esposito

The September 11, 2001 attacks on New York's World Trade Center and the Pentagon in Washington, DC reinforced the voices of those who warn of a clash of civilizations and the export of a 'fundamentalist' holy war to America and Europe. The threat of global terrorism and continued attacks by Islamist extremists continue to be portrayed as but the latest iteration of centuries-old confrontation and conflict between Islam and Christianity, the Muslim world and the West.

The Cold War attitudes of the West towards communism have been replicated in the projection of a new global threat. The tendency of many governments, the media and political analysts is to conclude the existence of an inherently anti-western global Islamic threat, often ignoring the very conditions that contribute to the growth of extremism and terrorism. Governments in Tunisia, Algeria, Egypt, Turkey, Southeast Asia and Central Asia as well as Israel, India and China have used the danger of Islamic radicalism to attract American and European foreign aid and to deflect from the failures of their governments or the indiscriminate suppression of opposition movements, mainstream as well as extremists.

The United States has pursued a war against global terrorism, criticized at times by many of its allies in Europe and the Arab and Muslim worlds for its unilateralism. The American and European governments have moved quickly against suspected terrorists through a series of raids, arrests and imprisonment, as well by implementing anti-terrorism legislation and regulations. If some have accused western governments of a lack of sufficient vigilance prior to September 11, others argue that the risk post-September 11 is the erosion of long-cherished civil liberties.

The global nature of Islamist extremism, symbolized and embodied by al-Qa'eda, the geographic scope of extremist attacks as well as their cells in Europe and America, have underscored the transnational threat of extremism. At the same time, they raise many questions and issues regarding the relationship of extremism to mainstream Islam in Muslim countries and in the West. Azza Karam's *Transnational Political Islam* addresses many of the questions raised by the acts of violence and terror of Osama Bin Laden and al-Qa'eda and post-September 11 Islamist extremists, in particular those that concern the transnational nature of political Islam and its European connections. Karam and her colleagues tackle a range of issues from the most fundamental to the more specific. What is political Islam? What is its relationship to violence and terror? Can one distinguish between Islamist extremism and mainstream Islam? What is the blowback effect? Post-September 11, how are Europeans coping with the integration of Muslims on the one hand, and the pursuit of international terrorist groups and their linkages and cells in Europe on the other? Are there moderate voices to be found in contemporary Islamic discourse?

Events post-September 11 have made it clear that the threat of global terror continues internationally and domestically, from attacks in Yemen and Bali to arrests – in Europe, America and Muslim countries – of those suspected of planning or carrying out acts of terrorism. At the same time, many charge that an 'imperial' America has too often used its overwhelming military and political power unilaterally, disproportionately and indiscriminately. As a result, across the Muslim world, the war against global terrorism is not seen as a war against extremists and terrorists but one against Islam and the Muslim world. Consequently, understanding the nature of transnational political Islam will remain a critical question in the Muslim world and in the West.

John Esposito
July 2003

1
Transnational Political Islam and the USA: An Introduction

Azza Karam

On September 11, 2001 two planes flew into the World Trade Center in New York City within minutes of each other. Soon after, a wing of the Pentagon in Washington DC (reportedly where key defence personnel were stationed) was also hit by a passenger plane. For the first time in history, planes full of civilians were being used as lethal weapons. A bearded figure in a white turban was flashed on TV screens across the world – Osama Bin Laden. In the words of the US media, this was the intelligence agencies' 'most wanted' man, the one who had allegedly masterminded the whole event and the many more to follow.

The first statements made by US President George W. Bush immediately after the World Trade Center attacks characterized the events as an 'attack on freedom' and 'on [American] values'. The intelligence sources of the world's most powerful nation would have us believe that this one man masterminded the collapse of the world's financial centre and the death of thousands purely on the basis of 'evil' and/or hatred. Bin Laden referred to these events as a response to (if not retaliation against) 'the triumph of the unjust over weak victims' (*nasrul-thalim 'alal mustad 'affien*), alluding to the US and Muslim regimes as the unjust, and citing Lebanon, Palestine and the children of Iraq, among others, as the victims.

Nearly one hour after they were hit, the symbols of the world's global trade centres, with innocents trapped inside and around, came crashing to the grounds. The targeted Pentagon section – the centre of military might – was gutted, and another plane had crashed in Pennsylvania. According to the news media, had this latter plane reached its destination – the White House itself, the symbol of global political power – that too would have borne the scars of a massive attack.

If indeed we are to believe that this apparent targeting of economic, political and military strongholds was perpetrated in the

1

name of evil, then what could have caused such hatred? Or was this, as the insinuation seems to indicate, a congenital state of mind or an inherent feature of the entire faith tradition? Evil, like beauty, is pretty much in the eyes of the beholder. To explain away major catastrophes in such terms is to view the world in binary terms of black and white: the forces of good/justice versus those of evil/injustice. It is, at best, simplistic. And yet this is the discourse employed by the US administration as well as its nemesis, al-Qa'eda.

This book presents some of the political dynamics underlying the violence perpetrated in the name of Islam against western interests. Rather than arguing for or against the Islamic faith, or attempting to explain the politics of Islamic societies as a whole, or analysing the structure of 'terrorist' organizations,[1] the chapters in this volume focus on the intersection of politics and Islam (political Islam, or Islamism) as it evolves in the lesser known parts of the western world. Largely, but not solely, drawing on unique European contexts, the presentations provide a comparative analysis of the social, economic and cultural dynamics within which Islamism does – or does not – develop.

Essentially, the chapters answer the following question: What is Islamism and how do Muslims living in parts of the western world interact with or relate to it – if at all?

To that end, this volume combines an unorthodox mix of western countries at different stages, some during important moments of transition, but all dealing with the politics of the right in one form or another. The countries selected in this volume are based on the following criteria:

1. Those (relatively) less dealt with in other English research/studies on their Muslim communities and the political dimension of their existence; hence Germany, France and the Netherlands.
2. Countries that are largely 'Islamic' in population but not necessarily so in culture, and in which the aspect of Islam plays an important role in their processes of socio-economic transition (hence Albania).

While the United States boasts the Christian Coalition, mainland European countries in the 1990s and the first two years of the twenty-first century have hosted the re-emergence of rightist political thought – the kind championed by Jean-Marie Le Pen in France and Pim Fortyn in the Netherlands. Even where the star of the respective figureheads faded, much of their political rhetoric, which appealed to some of their economically disaffected populations, was incorporated into mainstream political discourse. Germany post-unification; France in the midst of and just after parliamentary elections; Sweden dealing with the legacy of decades of social democracy and facing its increasingly vocal and visible Muslim populations; Albania post-communism with the political expediency of both Islamic rhetoric as well as its dire economic situation; and the Netherlands just before and after it dabbled with right-wing 'Fortynism'.[2] While this first chapter traces the structure, presents the rationale and outlines the transnational dynamics of Islamism, the last chapter critically analyses the discourse of Islamists through their writings in a renowned Islamist journal, *Al-Manar al-Jadid* (The New Lighthouse).

On God and Binary Thinking: Understanding the Discourse of the Bush Administration and al-Qa'eda

George W. Bush's binary 'you are either with us or against us' perspective is intimately connected to US foreign policy, which, for better or worse, determines a great deal of contemporary international relations. This view is an almost synchronized echo of Bin Laden's own message and way of thinking. According to Bin Laden, Muslims have undergone many years of injustice at the hands of '*Amrika*' (the USA) and its allies, and events such as those of September 11, 2001 are a repercussion or a retaliation. Both these views, ostensibly in direct opposition to each other, lay claim to righteousness and justice (or just action), emanating from a perception of 'injury'.

Interestingly, both men refer to 'God' many times. At the same time that Bin Laden was calling on and swearing to Allah, George W. Bush was referring to Psalm 23 and calling on God in his Address to the Nation. This prompts some to wonder whose side 'God' is on. And, perhaps more significantly, why bring God into this in the first place? The latter question will be dealt with in the conclusion to this chapter.

Regardless of whether or not Bin Laden did carry out the September 11 attacks,[3] his words (through his statement on the Arabic equivalent of CNN – Al-Jazeera television) clearly belie a process of quid pro quo: what is happening in the US is in response to the Palestinian issue, the presence of US troops on 'the Prophet

Muhammad's land' and Iraqi children. In the same breath that Bin Laden praised the attacks on the United States, he also critiqued the Muslim regimes currently in power. These regimes, he said, 'were quick to condemn the death of Americans, but far less vocal when it came to the deaths of their own citizens'. His message was not only delivered against 'Americans', but was a simultaneous threat to existing regimes in the Middle East – those that maintain the status quo and ally themselves with the United States – with a clear allusion to the Saudi regime in particular.

As the leading figure in an international Islamist configuration, Bin Laden (speaking for al-Qa'eda) is decisively linking people and events in parts of the Muslim world[4] with decisions and situations in the western hemisphere. According to this way of thinking, one set of events is intimately bound up with the other. The fact that national boundaries, and indeed spatial ones (land and sea), are being superseded, determines what is 'transnational' in this process.[5] And the use of 'Islam' to explain and legitimize political discourse and consequent action underlines the Islamist element.

Interestingly, the word al-Qa'eda in Arabic means 'the basis', hence, this could be a reference to a further structure for which this movement is but a base. The implication, therefore, is that what we see is not all there is. This certainly seems to be the approach of the current Bush Administration, which blames each and every attack or suspected attack on the seemingly endless network of al-Qa'eda.

But al-Qa'eda can also mean the rule and/or the norm according to which ideas, grammar, behaviour, etc. are organized. Hence what operates within this movement (or group or network) is what sustains a way of thinking and is the norm for behaviour, attitudes and action. Unlike the names of most other Islamist groups, this one is neither a noun (such as al-Jama'a, the group, or al-Ikhwan, the brotherhood) nor a verb (such as Jihad, to struggle, or Islah, to correct). This kind of basis, norm or rule knows no barriers and recognizes no borders (national or otherwise) – this is *the* foundation, *the* principle.

What is Political Islam? The Continuum

> The Prophet is our Leader, Islam is our Ideology, and the Holy Qur'an is our Constitution.[6]

Before beginning to look at the diversity of political Islam, it is important to stress that this is only one stream of politics within and outside the Muslim world. In fact, this is but a fraction of the different forms of social and political mobilization that take place among Muslims in general – and certainly amongst Muslim communities in the western hemisphere, as the chapters in this volume demonstrate.

Repeated statements by George W. Bush and other members of his Administration immediately after the events of September 11, and repeated by European leaders such as Britain's Tony Blair, France's Jacques Chirac and Germany's Gerhard Schroeder, highlight that the 'war against terrorism' has nothing to do with Islam. And yet 'Islamic extremism', 'Islamic terror', 'Islamic militants' and 'Islamic violence' have entered the mainstream lexicon.

Various authors have analysed political Islam (Olivier Roy, John Esposito, James Piscatori, Fred Halliday, Martin Marty and Scott Appleby, Abdel Malek, Augustus R. Norton, Anoush Ehteshami and Abdel Salam Sidahmed, Bassam Tibi, John O. Voll, Shireen Hunter and Emmanuel Sivan, to mention but a few). Often, terms such as Islamic fundamentalism, *salafi* and even Islamic radicalism have been used to explain the roots and objectives of all these movements. Much debate took place, particularly in the late 1980s and 1990s, about appropriate nomenclature. Suffice it here to say that the term Islamism is considered more appropriate to describe a continuum of movements which have a quintessentially political agenda, revolving around Islamizing (presumably rendering more Islamic) the structures of governance and the overall society.

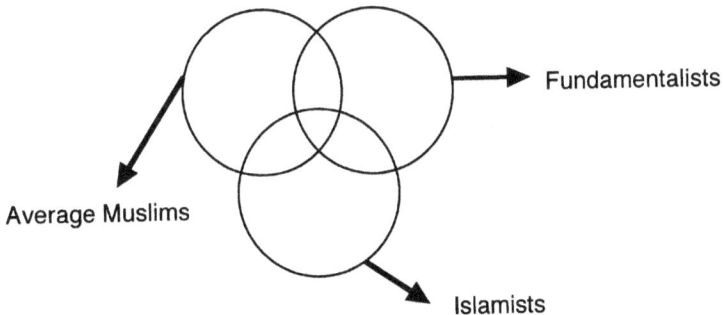

Figure 1

An Islamist is to be distinguished (see Figure 1) from her/his fundamentalist counterpart, in that s/he is not literal in her/his interpretations and understanding of text, and in fact can be quite creative in the manner in which s/he implements her/his 'religious' understanding. Also unlike fundamentalists, Islamists see religion as a primary motor for their work, but this work is rarely perceived as a 'spiritual' quest, nor is it only an attempt to become more religious in their personal or public lives.

Whereas a fundamentalist may or may not become engaged in political thought, debate and activism, an Islamist, by definition, does. Political engagement is the *sine qua non* of being an Islamist. The latter distinction also clarifies the difference between an Islamist, a Muslim fundamentalist and an average Muslim. In other words, it is the involvement in a movement or a group that is advocating or struggling for political change – specifically to render more 'Islamic' the social and/or political governing principles (or government) – that is the principal hallmark of an Islamist.

For many, including Osama Bin Laden, Islamic means just. In other words, a proper Islamic order, or context, is a just one. Clearly, however, what constitutes justice for some may not necessarily be just for all. Thus, to be an Islamist it is by no means sufficient to be a Muslim, nor is it even sufficient (or even necessary) to be a fundamentalist; rather, an Islamist must be committed to active engagement in the quest for a more Islamic and just society. All Islamists will share this ultimate aim.[7]

But what constitutes an 'Islamic' (or just) society, or Islamic governance? And what methods should be used to achieve this? These are the two key questions around which Islamists will differ (often radically) from each other. There is no homogeneous Islamist entity. It cannot be stressed enough that to see all Islamists as alike, and lump them all together as either 'fundamentalists', 'fanatics' or 'terrorists', is to obscure the significant differences within Islamist political thought and praxis. Indeed, when thinking of Islamist movements, one should think of a continuum, which in itself is a constantly changing kaleidoscope (see Figure 2). At the left end of the continuum is the 'moderate' tendency, while at the right lie more radical/extremist/militant tendencies. Clearly, these are generalized and relative political categories (the moderate can only be described as such when juxtaposed with the extremist, and vice versa). It is important to bear in mind that where the different groups and organizations fall on the continuum (as moderate or radical) is a matter of great debate and perception, not only among those outside the movements, but also within them.

The moderates[8] maintain that change will come about only through long-term education, social action, constituency building and advocacy, whereby increasing numbers of people become 'followers' and eventually espouse the political ideology-cum-social action package. Moderates will generally advocate and participate in elections, and in several Muslim countries where this is permitted,[9] they will register as political parties and organize themselves as such. One notable difference between Islamist parties and other political entities is that the moderate Islamists tend to have relatively well-defined social agenda(s), often exemplified by their provision of important social services (e.g. schools and clinics) in their respective communities. The latter lends them credibility and support among the various social classes (particularly the larger poorer ones) and thus constitutes an important factor in their political outreach and popularity.

Moderate Islamists are themselves very diverse in terms of their aims and agendas, as well as the modality of their organization. It may well be that one moderate party, at certain times during its interaction and existence, or on specific issues, adopts a stance that belongs more to the 'radical' end of the continuum. The Egyptian Muslim Brotherhood, for example, remained relatively silent during a spate of attacks against foreign tourists in Egypt carried out by radical Islamists. The Algerian FIS was radicalized after the Algerian elections (which they were expected to win) were cancelled by the intervention of the army in the early 1990s.

Alternatively, some radical Islamists may veer towards the moderate end of the continuum on specific issues or at certain times. An example of the latter is the Lebanese Hizbollah (Party of Allah), which has a history of anti-Israeli struggle and became notorious during the 1980s for the kidnapping of westerners in Beirut. In the 1990s, Hizbollah formed itself into a legitimate, recognized political party, ran for elections and won seats in the Lebanese parliament. Their decision to participate in electoral politics was certainly based on *realpolitik*,[10] but it was also a choice for a moderate strategy. Such a shift has implications for whether or not (and how) shari'a[11] should be applied.

Similarly, the Egyptian Jihad has announced a change in its policies with the renunciation of violence as a means to their envisaged end of an Islamic state. This renunciation began to take place after the massacre of tourists at Luxor, and the ensuing anger on the part of Egyptians, many of whom depend on the industry for their livelihoods and were thus adversely affected by the significant drop in revenues. Jihad's announcement was treated scathingly by

Ayman al-Zawahri (Bin Laden's right-hand man, al-Qa'eda ideologue and former leader of the movement), but it nevertheless was conveyed by the still imprisoned members through their lawyer in Cairo. By so doing, Jihad is attempting to move towards the more moderate, or left, end of the political continuum.

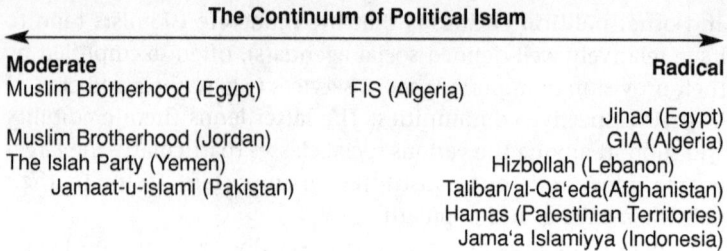

The Continuum of Political Islam

←——————————————————————————————————→

Moderate		Radical
Muslim Brotherhood (Egypt)	FIS (Algeria)	
		Jihad (Egypt)
Muslim Brotherhood (Jordan)		GIA (Algeria)
The Islah Party (Yemen)		Hizbollah (Lebanon)
Jamaat-u-islami (Pakistan)		Taliban/al-Qa'eda(Afghanistan)
		Hamas (Palestinian Territories)
		Jama'a Islamiyya (Indonesia)

Figure 2

While moderate Islamists stress that change will come about gradually, peacefully and with mass support, radical Islamists are Machiavellian in so far as they see violence as a (legitimate) means to an end. While they may sometimes justify it as a form of self-defence, radical Islamists will generally maintain that violence is both retaliatory and pre-emptive of more violence and aggression to come. This is evidenced by Bin Laden's insinuation that by targeting the US and other western nations as unjust powers (*thalim*), what is taking place is retaliation against western actions, a triumph by the injured and a pre-emption of future injustices. Especially since the US stepped up its rhetoric on their need to wage war against Iraq, taped speeches sent by radical Islamists have contained warnings of more violence to come. This is not to say that if the US had abstained from going to war with Iraq, radical Islamists would have halted their cycle of violence. The acts of terror which are taking place today by radical Islamists are seen as a reaction to US hegemony and actions which have already taken place.

The Palestinian–Israeli Conflict, Democracy, Human Rights and Common Platforms with Non-Islamist Muslim Politics

Islamists and other parties in the Muslim world at large share common political platforms, in addition to general concerns involved with poverty and globalization. Almost all political parties in the Arab Muslim world are pro-Palestinian, emotively and intellectually. Regardless of whether they are Muslim, Christian or agnostic, all political parties, even those traditionally at odds and enemies of one another on other aspects, see Israel as an occupier of Palestinian land. Interestingly, however, it is because the most vociferous supporters of the Palestinians have been Islamists (dating back to the large contingent of Muslim Brotherhood members who fought alongside the Palestinians in 1948) that the issue of Palestine is seen and presented as 'Islamic' – as though there are no Christian Palestinians. This distortion of reality has contributed to the widespread misinterpretation and evocation of the Arab–Israeli conflict as though it were a Muslim–Jewish one. This in turn feeds into current rhetoric employed by the Sharon administration in Israel, that it is 'also' fighting a war against (Islamic) terrorists. In the words of one Syrian (Orthodox) scholar, Palestinian Christians are in 'double jeopardy – not only do they suffer as all Palestinians [do] under occupation, but they do not even exist in their struggle'.

Those Arab ruling parties that have signed peace treaties with Israel (and non-Arab political parties in Muslim countries) continue to maintain (quoting international law and various UN resolutions) that the Israeli presence in Gaza and the West Bank constitutes an occupation, and that Israel should agree to East Jerusalem becoming the capital of a Palestinian state.

Islamists, moderate and radicals alike, tend to disagree with their political counterparts on whether peace and normalization of relations with Israel is wise and/or necessary. Radical Islamists will argue that Israel's very presence and existence is in itself a constant act of aggression against the Palestinians and as such should be resisted. The precise forms that resistance should take (and what constitutes 'legitimate' armed struggle) is a matter of discussion and debate. However, during the two Palestinian Intifadas, Islamists across the Muslim world have been arguably among the most vocal and active in their solidarity with the Palestinian cause. On suicide bombings, moderate Islamists have joined with their radical counterparts to counter mainstream Islamic voices[12] by stating that as long as the targets are Israeli soldiers, the suicides are a legitimate form of struggle. Most radical Islamists, however, maintain that the suicide bombings are a legitimate form of self-defence against ongoing Israeli aggression, and thus effectively do not distinguish between Israeli military and civilian populations.

Significantly, matters relating to advocacy for democracy and human rights are also shared by Islamist and non-Islamist parties in many parts of the Muslim world, with the exception of countries where Islamists are the ruling regimes and either fraught with internal dissension on how to implement an 'Islamic democracy' (e.g. Iran), or unwilling to contemplate and/or engage – publicly – in such discussions (e.g. Saudi Arabia). Those opposed to Islamists heatedly maintain that Islamist espousal of democracy is opportunistic (a means to achieve power themselves after which they will eliminate it), citing Khomeini and events prior to and after the Iranian revolution of 1979.

As for championing human rights, anti-Islamists will claim the motivation behind that centres on the fact that Islamists themselves are victims of human rights abuses that certain regimes perpetrate. Once in power, they maintain, Islamists will have no qualms about perpetrating the same abuses against their opponents. These sceptical voices can now be heard in Pakistan following the success there of the Islamist parties in the 2001 parliamentary elections.

Islamism in the West: Religion, Politics, the US and 'Blowback'?

But what of Islamism in the western world? Even the paranoia characteristic of the George W. Bush Administration falls short of believing that Islamists want to 'Islamize' western governments and/or society. And, indeed, political Islam has different priorities when it operates in the western hemisphere. Rather than seeking to Islamize the state, Islamists see western governments, particularly the United States, as being the main props of corrupt and illegitimate regimes in various Islamic countries. In addition, they view western countries, in particular the United States, as the principal backers of the state of Israel.

From an economic perspective, the same arguments articulated by the anti-globalization movement, i.e. that these western countries are exploiting the poorer ones, and continue to use free trade to oppress their peoples to maintain their global hegemony, are echoed by Islamists. Yet it has become abundantly clear, after the fall of the Berlin Wall and the collapse of the Soviet Union, and particularly after the events of September 11, 2001 and the play of world politics, that the US is the only global hegemon. As such, it is perceived as the main source of difficulties and problems in the Islamic world.

From the oil-fields of Saudi Arabia and Kuwait to the jungles of Sri Lanka, the United States has a palpable presence – if not military, then political and/or economic – in the world's smallest nooks and crannies. Barber (1996) refers to this economic hegemony as 'McWorld', while Robertson (1992), Waters (1995) and others refer to aspects of this as the 'globalization' of American influence. On the other hand, 'protecting [their] national interest' is a common – and honest – refrain of many a US Administration, including the various plays the Bush Administration makes on 'making the world safe for our children'.

There are many 'interests' that the US would seek to protect, and few of them are spared the cynical perception of many of the world's inhabitants. The US is seen by many in the developing world in general, and by Islamists in particular, as the modern-day imperialist, with all the incumbent baggage of anger and resentment this engenders. When referring to Islamism, this attitude is often interpreted as hatred of 'the West' and even of 'modernity'.

When it comes to acknowledging the extent of US involvement and/or interest in the Muslim world, the list is long and laborious, especially taking into account the direct presence of US military personnel, along with the various economic, social and cultural projects, programmes and institutions. For many in the Muslim world, the US employs a double standard when dealing with certain Muslim countries, as evidenced in the recent débâcle over Iraq. Ordinary Muslims (Arabs and non-Arab) and non-Muslim Arabs are today asking: why was the United States so insistent that the Iraqi regime comply with all the United Nations resolutions, when Israel seems to be able to get away with non-compliance? And why is it that despite the fact that North Korea has admitted to having nuclear weapons, the North Korean regime is known to be anything but democratic and it has been identified as part of the 'Axis of Evil' by George W. Bush, the United States was still intent on bombing Iraq while relying on diplomacy with North Korea? For Islamists this is a clear indication that the United States is intent on fighting Islam in much the same way it did the Soviet Union and communism. Needless to say, this image is reinforced by what is perceived as the continuous turning of a blind eye to the Israeli Administration's 'preventive action'/retaliation against hundreds of Palestinian civilians in response to the suicide bombings.

Indeed, there are many theories that purport a historical antagonism (or struggle) between the 'West' (sometimes represented by the US) and the 'Islamic/Muslim' world (Huntington, 1993; Emerson, 2002; Kramer, 1997). But the resentment felt by the Islamists vis-à-vis the United States is not a matter that requires much delving into. Instead, radical Islamism (such as that seen in the acts of September 11, 2001) is quite simply captured in the term adopted by Chalmers Johnson: 'blowback'.

> The term 'blowback', which officials of the Central Intelligence Agency first invented for their own use ... refers to the unintended consequences of policies that were kept secret from the American people. What the daily press reports as the malign acts of 'terrorists' or 'drug lords' or 'rogue states' or 'illegal arms merchants' often turn out to be blowback from earlier American operations. (Johnson, 2001: 8)

There is ample evidence to indicate that present-day 'terrorists'(e.g. the Taliban) or Saddam Hussein and the former Iraqi regime are all former 'friends' of the United States. In some instances, they were supported and sustained financially and militarily by the US. Still lacking from the official rhetoric of the US regime is why (and at what point) did the former 'good guys' become 'bad guys'. Whatever the explanation for the change of heart, there is one good analogy for this form of blowback which 'happened' to one of the regimes in the Middle East, which is both a regional leader and a close US ally: Egypt.

In the early 1970s, the late Egyptian President Anwar al-Sadat came to power (following the death of the charismatic socialist and Arab nationalist leader Gamal Abdel Nasser). One of Sadat's key concerns was to attempt to counter the overriding popularity of Nasser's socialist ideology. As a means to achieve this, he freed some of the Islamists imprisoned under the Nasser regime and turned a blind eye to their attempts to regroup. Eventually, Sadat's capitalism, which seemed to benefit only a tiny elite, paled in comparison to Islamist ideology, the latter made more popular by the provision and management of an extensive network of social services to Egypt's most economically disenfranchised. And yet when he turned against Islamists and all political opposition in his famous political 'purge' of September 1980, Sadat only succeeded in enraging the population. Finally, on 6 October 1981, Sadat was murdered by precisely the same forces he had unleashed and then attempted to 'contain'. His assassination was part of the blowback against his own actions and those of his regime.

It is at best risky to believe that control can be maintained once individuals have espoused an ideology about the implementation of 'God's rule'. And yet it is remarkable how many regimes and individuals will do just that, either to gain or consolidate power, whether locally or internationally – including several US Administrations. The formation of Jerry Falwell's Moral Majority in 1979, which was the formalization of what today is referred to as the Christian Coalition, or the religious right, signalled a situation where the entry of the religious into the political arena becomes common practice in contemporary and supposedly secular US dynamics. As Terence Samuel (2002) writes in an article on the United States:

> [T]he evangelical movement is firmly entrenched in the nation's political life, lobbying and leveraging like any of the hundreds of other pressure groups in Washington out to advance their causes and promote their issues. The Christian Coalition's Web site is a beehive of political advocacy, and not just on traditional issues like abortion and school prayer ... the Coalition worked doggedly on behalf of GOP candidates during the last election and might well take credit for swinging the Senate.

Urging the US Administration to deeper and more active involvement in Muslim countries (from supporting the Christian – and animist – South in the civil war in the Sudan, to assisting Israel by returning all the Jewish peoples to Jerusalem and the Promised Land in order to hasten the second coming of Christ), the legacy of the Coalition and its like-minded allies can (and does) contribute to the violent blowback the US has witnessed and will continue to witness.

In fact, one can argue that the course this US Administration has currently embarked on (the war on terror in Afghanistan, the war in Iraq) has served only to bolster the legitimacy and credibility of Islamism as a whole. Now, not only the US but increasingly Russia is perceived to be totally opposed to Islam, and since current regimes cannot and do not appear to be able to resist, Islamists have profiled themselves as 'heroes' – defenders of Islam and Muslim nations. But radical Islamist terror is also increasingly seen as 'understandable' by many desperate people. Interviewing several Chechens soon after the hostage-taking in Moscow, LaFraniere (2002) noted:

> After years amid Grozny's heaps of rubble, open fires and charred, windowless apartment houses, many Chechens say they

consider desperate acts to end the war not just understandable but inevitable.

The rise of the Muslim religious right during the most recent elections in Pakistan is a direct result of the alliance of Pakistan's Parvez Musharraf and the US, post-September 11, 2001. Indeed, the contention is that were democratic elections to be held in many parts of the Arab Muslim world tomorrow, the Islamist parties would win on an 'anti-US, pro-Islam' ticket alone.

But the Islamist victors in Pakistan were keen to clarify their stance as pro-democracy and as supporters of women (i.e. distinguishing themselves from their Afghan Taliban radical co-religionists). Throughout their campaigns and soon after the announcement of the election results, they were emphasizing their Islamist credentials, while making clear their opposition to US policy in the Muslim world. Radical Islamism, at best a thin sliver of the Islamist political tendency (but the one with the most devastating bite), can be considered part of the blowback against the United States.

It must be stressed, however, that it is misleading to view Islamism as a whole as a blowback against US policy. Moderate Islamism has a different trajectory which renders it necessary to distance itself from acts of terror. Such acts have in the past seriously delegitimized Islamism within and outside of the Muslim world.[13]

The Structure of the Book

In this volume, Hamzawy traces competing and often contradictory tendencies within the thinking of moderate Islamists by reviewing their journal, *Al-Manar al-Jadid*, published in Egypt and widely distributed around the Arab world. While not directly critiquing the blowback theory, Hamzawy highlights the 'possible normative isolation' of radical Islamism, and sees it as a hopeful sign that some Muslims may look to their own shortcomings rather than 'blame the West' for their ills.

But what of the Islamist context in the West? Hjärpe, speaking of Sweden, and Amiraux referring to Bosnian and Turkish Muslims in Germany and France, deal with some aspects of this trajectory. Attempting to mobilize Muslim communities abroad as a constituency that can support – financially, intellectually and, as reported, through the phenomenon of 'sleepers' – certain Islamist movements in their home country is not uncommon. But Amiraux demonstrates how even a secular government such as Turkey's seeks to maintain its links with Turkish Muslim immigrants abroad by training imams and ensuring a presence in the leadership of the various organizations in Germany. Hjärpe, on the other hand, begins by clearly rejecting the argument that political Islam can play a role in Sweden, indicating that Muslim organizations which wish to benefit from state subsidies cannot risk being political as such. However, he then alludes to how Sweden's welfare policies and a changing sense of 'belonging' among Muslims can create a void in which a moderate version of Islamism may develop.

Hjärpe maintains that dominant social and political frameworks – those exercised by the (Swedish) state – which control the flow of resources, together with the inevitable generational gap that develops among immigrants, is bound to act as a buffer against the development of radical political Islam. Amiraux argues in similar vein while tracing the development of Turkish and Kurdish groups, and contrasts that with Bosnian groups in Germany. She is meticulous in underlining how moments of crisis in 'countries of origin' (the countries from where Muslim immigrants to Europe originate) can form a catalyst not only for groups mobilizing along identity lines and willing to integrate into their host countries, but also for those who are organizing along political lines against the status quo, i.e. Islamists. The gist of their argument is that whether in Sweden or in Germany, a strong tendency towards individualization means that a more 'individualized' and European Islam has developed, which may miligate against the emergence of a collectivist radical Islamist movement. This argument is furthered to some extent by Nederveen Pieterse in his chapter on the Netherlands, in which he highlights the interrelatedness between the Muslim community and events occurring in Muslim countries, but also argues that there is too much diversity within and among Muslims in the Netherlands to enable a mass movement of political Islam – let alone one that justifies the use of violence.

Thus, Nederveen Pieterse, Amiraux and Hjärpe all maintain that whereas a diverse European Islamic culture is evolving, with some degree of identity based on Islam emerging, a radical political ideology – such as that of al-Qa'eda – is not. They do point out in different ways that the secular nature of governance in Europe can translate into the greater liklihood of Islam being 'instrumentalized' by certain groups, and that this situation is profoundly aggravated by crises unfolding in the Muslim world. Nevertheless, they also indicate that even where moderate Islamism manifests itself, it is balanced by what Amiraux refers to as a 'transnational belonging'.

A different European context is described by Frederick Abrahams, writing on Albania. Illustrating a society emerging from its own fair share of poverty and repression, Abrahams stresses how the regime's leadership, after the Soviet era, is vulnerable to the influence not only of certain Islamic governments, but also to the activities of certain organizations, some of which have a dubious lineage. Whereas Swedish, Dutch, French and German societies have a degree of individualization which may protect them against radical Islamist thought and action, and have governments that are (democratically) strong and centralized, Albania has over-disintegrated in such a way that religion is not so much a feature of identity (local or trans-national) as a tool to bring in much needed resources – whether for an individual priest-turned-imam, or for a government.

When this chapter was being written, the US Congress approved a resolution authorizing the use of force in Iraq, despite the Iraqi government agreeing to allow in UN weapons inspectors and repeatedly indicating that no conditions were attached to this. During the time the resolution was being debated, yet another tape featuring Bin Laden and his associate, Ayman al-Zawahri, was released by Al-Jazeera. This time, the wording was unambiguous: US action would have consequences. Several French engineers were killed in Karachi by a suicide car bomb. A French oil tanker has been blown up in Yemeni waters, and more than 150 people, including many Australian, British, and French citizens, killed in a bomb blast on Bali. After decades of poor performance in general elections, both the Pakistani and the Moroccan Islamist parties have increased their vote in the latest elections. Is all this pure coincidence, or are we witnessing a blowback?

In the Muslim world, Islamism is a multifaceted attempt to transform the ruling regime(s) and societies into a more Islamic, and allegedly just, reality. In the western contexts, where moderate Islamism has yet to appear relevant, pockets of radical Islamists are also intent on some form of 'justice'. Whereas there is nothing to justify the murders of hundreds of innocent civilians, is it conceivable that such Islamists have their own version of 'collateral damage'? If indeed this appears to be the case, then will the current strategy of the US-led 'war against terrorism' succeed in eradicating terrorism, or will it merely further the *raison d'être* of radical Islamists who already believe that this is a war against Islam and Muslims? In other words, are we witnessing the age of repeated blowbacks?

The current US administration would have us believe that by invading Iraq and ousting its ruler, the hand that feeds terror and the terrorist sword of Damocles (in the form of biological and chemical weapons capabilities) will be controlled, and the world made safe. At the same time, we are told that al-Qa'eda is composed of many unknown cells, each with its own agenda, and few of them known or controllable. To the former argument, the only answer can be that this sounds very much like what was earlier maintained about Afghanistan, and whereas there will undoubtedly be relief in many parts of Afghanistan at the end of Taliban rule, there is little evidence that terrorism has been eradicated. As Seumas Milne (2002) maintains:

> After a year of US military operations in Afghanistan and around the world the CIA director George Tenet conceded that the threat from al-Qaida and associated jihadist groups was as serious as before September 11. In other words the global US onslaught had been a failure – at least as far as dealing with non-state terrorism is concerned.

Al-Qa'eda has indeed not been contained in Afghanistan, nor is it likely to be contained in, by or through the war in Iraq. Transnational bases, or rules, are not about to be eradicated by conventional weapons. Therefore, every act of war currently undertaken by the US government – no matter how justified it may seem – is likely to engender one response, many times over: blowback.

Futures: The Gender Dimension and Religious Discourse(s)

What has predominated thus far is a discourse of war articulated through a diverse array of men. Prior to the invasion of Afghanistan, the US media was inundated with news and documentaries about the oppressive conditions that Afghan women were undergoing under the Taliban regime. It seems to have escaped the notice of this vast media machine that the Taliban were in power for years before September 11, 2001 – and none of these years was any different for Afghan women. Nevertheless, the impression given was that the western world was not only going into Afghanistan to eradicate terrorism, but was also on its way to liberate oppressed Afghani Muslim women.

Interestingly, this is the same argument that former colonial powers have articulated as a way to legitimize their presence in any country. Leila Ahmed (1992) demonstrates this in her seminal work on *Women and Gender in Islam*, and gives as an example Lord Cromer during British colonial rule in Egypt. According to Ahmed, Cromer cited the 'backward' condition of Muslim women as a means to justify in part why it was that the British had a civilizing mission to undertake in Egypt. So why is this relevant to transnational political Islam?

The clamour within the US establishment to 'support' Afghan women, which drew in notable women politicians, including Hillary Clinton, Laura Bush and Lynn Cheney, and crossed the Atlantic to be supported by Britain's Cherie Booth, all worked to underline the argument that the great civilizing mission of the western world includes, as a significant part of its mandate, the 'liberation' of Muslim women.[14] And yet Muslim women, in all their diversity and forms of activism, have been insistent that this is not necessarily the kind of assistance they require from their western sisters and brothers. The story of a former Afghan Minister for Social Affairs illustrates why this rhetoric is unhelpful for women. One of only two women in the male-dominated Cabinet, and one of the few who was vocal in criticizing the way family laws denied women their basic rights, she was forced to resign her post as a result of the attacks directed against her by conservative religious spokespersons.

The former minister feared for her life in view of the allegations she was taunted with – allegations that are made against many a women's rights activist in the Muslim world: that she was a lackey of the West and was against Islam – a hair's breadth away from being a heretic. As such, she was seen as a dangerous influence in Afghan society. She now heads an independent Commission on Human Rights, and a new government has lost a capable woman in a position of authority who had vowed to work to improve the track record on women's human rights in Afghanistan.

The allegations levelled against this women's rights activist – pro-West/anti-Islam – are often synonymous, are not only levelled against women and, in some cases, can indeed be life-threatening. Towards the end of the 1990s, a Cairo university professor, Nasr Hamid Abu Zeid, was accused of apostasy for daring to argue, among other things, that the interpretation of certain texts in the Qur'an required contextualization. Resurrecting an old law, Islamist lawyers filed a case against him, not only accusing him of apostasy, but demanding that he divorce his wife (since no Muslim woman is allowed to be married to a non-Muslim man). The case received much coverage, and since then, Abu Zeid has had to live in exile in order both to protect his life[15] and to remain married. What received less media attention, however, was that Abu Zeid was also a valuable resource and ally for women's rights activists in Egypt. To this day, Abu Zeid feels unable to return to his home country.

In other words, there is a gender dimension to the Islamist blowback and this is a flashback to the bad old days of colonialism. Activists for women's rights in the Muslim world, together with those intellectuals arguing for both moderate Islamic and secular political dynamics, are forever attempting to ward off criticisms from two sides:[16] the religious right in their own countries (for whom they are never 'authentic' or 'Islamic' enough) on the one hand, and the western right wing (seeing much of what takes place in the Muslim world as principally anti-western) on the other.

In view of the contemporary political context, both right-wing discourses are aggravated, which tightens the noose around moderate discourse – including advocacy for women's rights. In this situation, a backlash against women's rights discourse and, by implication, a 'third way' of thinking politically, socially, culturally and economically in the Muslim world and amongst Muslim communities, is muted. A vicious cycle is perpetrated: with the muted moderate discourse emerges a louder radical one, which in turn leads to further antagonisms and conflict.

In Lieu of a Conclusion

> Say no to racism. But don't stop there. Say no to sexism. But don't stop there. Say no to anti-Semitism and anti-Islamism. But don't stop there.
> (The Reverend Jesse Jackson, addressing the Rally against War with Iraq, Washington, DC, 26 October 2002)

In his concluding comments, Peter Bergen[17] notes: '[i]n the past al-Qaeda has carried its holy war from its base in Afghanistan to countries around the world. Now the world has carried that war back to al-Qaeda' (2002: 224). Bergen cites this as an example of the 'what goes around comes around' adage, indicating that Bin Laden now has more enemies than friends. While that is undoubtedly true, it mirrors what Bin Laden had been saying, that whatever they undertake in terms of (terrorist) activity, the US is reaping what it has sown. Accordingly, there is an anticipation that what the US has done in Afghanistan, and its recent war and regime change in Iraq, is also sowing the seeds of further conflict – especially as viewed from an Islamist perspective. This is a vicious cycle.

A former Secretary-General of NATO, Willy Claes, went on record in the 1990s for saying that after the collapse of communism, the new enemy was Islamic fundamentalism, or the 'green enemy'. Many students of Middle Eastern politics and Islam feared then that this would sow even greater seeds of distrust, war, even, among those in the Arab and Muslim worlds who already perceived an attempt by the West to dominate, manipulate and exploit the resources and wealth of that part of the world for their own interests.

Statements like Claes's were seen by many critics of US foreign policy in the Middle East and elsewhere as verbalizing the obvious: 'Islam' was being made the enemy. Sceptics still ask why the US and the West seek to vilify Islam. Some Islamists (and intellectuals on the left of the political spectrum) rationalize this as part of a global Zionist conspiracy, or, as one Islamist woman put it, 'Euro-Ameri-Zionism'.[18] For many others, the perception is that the former colonial powers, led by the US, are seeking to control the vast oil reserves from Saudi Arabia to Afghanistan, from Iran to the Central Asian Republics.

The argument is that where the US fails to manipulate governments (as it has done in Saudi Arabia, for example), they will 'manufacture' an excuse to demean and subjugate a country until they and their allies finally control its resources. Each and every interaction that involves engagement at some level with the western world is seen, by Islamists and leftists alike, largely from that perspective. This way of thinking leads to an advocacy of at best an economic and cultural boycott of all things western, and at worst a call for retaliation against this (continuing) western 'crusade'.

There are other voices, those of realists (so-called for the sake of description), in the Muslim world and elsewhere. Realists argue that the collapse of the Soviet Union has brought into sharper focus the actions of a dominant power, which in turn seeks to establish alliances to further its own interests. In other words, there is no conspiracy (or undeclared war) against any part of the world, but what is afoot is (political) business as usual. Rather than attempt to 'retaliate', or 'make war', this way of thinking advocates the need to cooperate and 'normalize' relations with the western world and their associates, including Israel. This is not simply an 'if you can't beat them join them' attitude, but is motivated primarily by a realization that constructive engagement is the only way to benefit from these unilateral dynamics. Many current regimes in the Middle East in particular espouse this view. Those opposed to these regimes, however, are also opposed to their apparently unquestioning alliance with the western world.

The Soviet Union has collapsed, and a unipolar world is a reality that is hard to escape. Traditional oppositions between nation-states are being replaced. Instead, non-state actors, such as the Chechens, Kurds, al-Qa'eda and others, are the opponents. Many of these actors are lumped together under the catch-all term 'terrorists', which provides a convenient category at once minimizing their differences and clarifying 'an enemy' to intelligence institutions still comfortable thinking in terms of binarisms. By rendering all Islamists enemies, and thus failing to see the distinctions between and among them, western countries risk furthering the image of themselves as crusaders against Islam, which in turn consolidates the perception that some Islamists maintain. What is perpetuated is therefore a vicious cycle where misperceptions feed on each other.

East and West are no longer worlds apart. They have, *pace* Kipling, already met. In fact, the essays in this volume testify that not only is there a varied European Islam, but also distinctive forms of transnational radical political Islam which are based not so much on Islamizing the state and implementing shari'a laws, but instead bent on 'justice' (or vengeance), for international acts perpetuated by a hegemonic nation and its allies. In a sense, the 'Wild West' tactics of 'you're either with us or against us' (and if you are against, then you will pay) seem to be ruling the roost on both sides of the so-called 'war against terrorism'.

It is ironic that religion, or self-proclaimed spokespersons of religion, feature strongly in these oppositional dynamics, whether on the side of the Bush regime or Bin Laden. Engaged political voices on the right of the religious spectrum seem to be louder than at any time in the twentieth or twenty-first centuries, whether in the US or the Muslim world. Clearly, religion can no longer be ignored. The question is, therefore, whether it is time to broaden the political space to include moderate religious voices. Secularism, understood as the so-called separation between church and state, is severely challenged. Could this be a window of opportunity for the religious peace-makers to intervene?

If an alternative articulation of religion could be heard in this cacophony of right-wing 'God talk', would it speak to the commonalities of culture and circumstance rather than the supposed clashes? Would it moderate the language of the US religious and political leadership, and mitigate against the sense of victimhood and injustice felt by al-Qa'eda's actual and potential supporters? Could an alternative religious discourse, which draws its legitimacy and inspiration from successes achieved by religious communities in their roles as peace-builders,[19] break the current impasse of violence?

I argued earlier that it is imperative to recognize the diversity between and among Islamists. I also maintain that not only is there a difference between moderate and radical Islamism – particularly with regard to the use of violence as a tactic to achieve their aims – but that some moderate Islamists find it counter-productive to be associated with terrorism. Yet I further maintain that current political dynamics are leading to a vigour amonge radical Islamists at the expense of moderate religious discourse.

So who could champion such a discourse and how? My contention here is that moderate Islamists may be more viable interlocutors than previously imagined (or desired). A sophisticated approach would be for those against the war in Iraq, or a Third World War, in both the US and other western administrations and civil society, to form strategic alliances with moderate Islamists, such as President Khatami of Iran. Such alliances would simultaneously raise the profile of moderate tendencies in the Islamic world itself (redressing the current clampdown), while providing legitimacy for the kind of moderate discourse that would see justice as a common goal for all.

Detractors, sceptics and hawks would baulk at this contention and question why western support should provide legitimacy for moderate religious discourse, when the same support seems to bolster angry Islamists around the world, as in Pakistan. The answer is that western support is currently provided by a bellicose western administration to administrations with questionable legitimacy in the Muslim world. Moderate Islamists are not to be equated with the latter.

A further question is why endorse or attempt to support any religious discourse when, clearly, the over-involvement of religion is part of the present-day dilemmas in the first place? The answer is two-fold. First, religion is here to stay. Furthermore, what is currently at play, whether in the West or the Islamic world, is a radical religious discourse, which sees violence as legitimate (whether it is labelled as self-defence against western interests or against 'Islamic terrorists'), harps on cultural clashes and is diametrically opposed to international conventions honouring women and children,[20] in the name of family values. This has to be distinguished from a religious discourse which spurns all violence and is prepared to work together towards a semblance of international social justice.

There are many more objections to this line of thinking, and yet, with the current dynamics unfolding and promising more fear and bloodshed, dare we ignore the possibilities and opportunities?

Notes

1. There is an increasing number of studies dealing with Muslims and/or Islam in the West, and a plethora on political Islam in the Muslim world. In the two years since September 11, 2001, the amount of research on 'Islamic terrorism' and the like has burgeoned. But contemporary comparative research on political Islam in the West is relatively scarce; hence the rationale behind this book.
2. A reference to Pim Fortyn, who is variously quoted as saying that 'Islam is a backward religion' and 'the Netherlands is full [enough]', i.e. does not need more immigrants. See Chapter 4 by Nederveen Pieterse.
3. It should be noted that there is a healthy scepticism among many Muslims, from South Africa to Saudi Arabia, with regard to Bin Laden's culpability, with several people claiming he was not responsible, but was using the opportunity of the events to express his opinions and rage.
4. This refers to countries where the majority population are Muslim and/or where the states identify themselves as such.
5. Indeed, General Schwarzkopf, immediately after September 11, said that before these attacks, the 'two oceans have been a sanctuary for [Americans] ... Terrorism came to our shores big time now' – a clear indication that US policy-makers felt that spatial boundaries had been definitively crossed. With that realization came a sense of insecurity and a desire to respond, so that the general was 'delighted to hear about [the President's] statement of going after those people [al-Qa'eda in Afghanistan]'.
6. The motto of the Muslim Brotherhood and like-minded Islamists.
7. Which partly explains why the relatively new Egyptian Islamist party al-Wasat, boasts a couple of Christian members.
8. An example of a moderate Islamist party in the Muslim world is the Muslim Brotherhood (al-Ikhwan al-Muslimin), which came into existence in 1928 in Egypt, and which has branched out in different countries since, and is very diverse in its structure and organizational method(s).
9. Lebanon, Jordan, Algeria, Indonesia, Malaysia, Pakistan, to name but a few.
10. An indication that the eventual withdrawal of Israeli troops from the south of Lebanon would lead to the questioning of the longevity of Hizbollah's claim to legitimacy.

11. Commonly translated as Islamic law, it is worth noting that shari'a is not one body of text or interpretation, but rather the sum of various juridical interpretations collated over a certain course of time. Thus, there is no one shari'a law, but a whole set of man-made laws – some of which may differ according to the specific school of interpretation followed. This would also partly explain why certain applications of shari'a differ from one Muslim country to another.

12. Such as the Mufti of Bosnia and the Sheikh of al-Azhar in Egypt, both of whom maintained that suicide is against Islam – even if the resistance to Israeli occupation is legitimate.

13. As referred to earlier in the aftermath of the Luxor massacre in Egypt and the massacres carried out by the GIA during the civil war in Algeria, for example.

14. For more on the emerging behaviour of the US empire, see George Monbiot's 'The Logic of Empire', in the *Guardian Weekly*, 15–20 August, p. 11; and Philip Golub's 'Westward the Course of Empire', in *Le Monde Diplomatique*, as quoted in the *Guardian Weekly*, 6 September 2002, p. 6.

15. Some of the radical Islamists maintain that it is legitimate to kill an apostate.

16. I have elaborated on the relationship between political Islam and women's activism and the manner in which a gender discourse is intimately connected to the power dynamics that take place between Islamist political thought and governmental reactions, in Karam (1998).

17. Author of what has become the *New York Times* bestseller, *Holy War, Inc.: The Secret World of Osama Bin Laden* (New York: Simon and Schuster, 2001, reprinted 2002).

18. See Karam (1998).

19. For more on this, see Johnston and Sampson (1994); Johansen (1997); Appleby (1999); Gopin (2000); Abu-Nimer (2001); Fox (2001); and Alger (2002).

20. It is interesting to note that whether it is the Christian Coalition of the US or radical Islamists such as the Taliban, both have serious problems with the United Nations as a viable entity, as well as with the Convention for the Elimination of All Forms of Discrimination Against Women (CEDAW) as well as the International Convention on the Child (ICC).

References

Abdel Salam, Sidhamed and Ehteshami, Anoush (eds.). *Islamic Fundamentalism* (Boulder, Colorado: Westview Press, 1996).

Abu-Nimer, Mohammed. 'Conflict Resolution, Culture and Religion: Towards a Training Model of Interreligious Peacebuilding', *Journal of Peace Research*, Vol. 38, No. 6, 2001, pp. 685–704.

Ahmad, Eqbal. *Terrorism: Theirs and Ours* (with a Foreword by David Barsamian) (New York: Seven Stories Press, 2001).

Ahmed, Leila. *Women and Gender in Islam: Historical Roots of a Modern Debate* (New Haven and London: Yale University Press, 1992).

Alger, Chadwick. 'Religion as a Peace Tool', *The Global Review of Ethnopolitics*, Vol. 1, No. 4, June 2002, pp. 94–109.

Armstrong, Karen. *Holy War: The Crusades and their Impact on Today's World* (New York: Anchor Books, 2001).

Appleby, Scott. *The Ambivalence of the Sacred: Religion, Violence and Reconciliation* (Boston: Rowan and Littlefeld, 1999).

Ayubi, Nazih. *Political Islam: Religion and Politics in the Arab World* (London: Routledge, 1991).

Barber, Benjamin R. *Jihad vs. McWorld: How Globalism and Tribalism Are Reshaping the World* (New York: Ballantine Books, 1996).

Belling, Willard A. (ed.). *The Middle East: Ten Years after Camp David* (Washington: The Brookings Institute, 1998).

Bergen, Peter. *Holy War, Inc.: Inside the Secret World of Osama Bin Laden* (New York: Simon and Schuster, 2002).

Choueiri, Youssef. *Islamic Fundamentalism* (London: Pinter Publishers, 1990).

Davis, G. Scott (ed.). *Religion and Justice in the War over Bosnia* (New York and London: Routledge, 1996).

do Ceu Pinto, Maria. *Political Islam and the United States: A Study of U.S. Policy towards Islamist Movements in the Middle East* (Reading: Garnet Publishing, 1999).

Efrat, Moshe and Bercovitch, Jacob (eds.). *Superpowers and Client States in the Middle East: The Imbalance of Influence* (London: Routledge, 1991).

Emerson, Steven. *American Jihad: The Terrorists Living Among Us* (New York: The Free Press, 2002).

Esposito, John. *The Islamic Threat: Myth or Reality?* (Oxford: Oxford University Press, 1992).

Eickelman, Dale F. and Piscatori, James. *Muslim Politics* (Princeton: Princeton University Press, 1996).

El-Said, Sabah. *Between Pragmatism and Ideology: The Muslim Brotherhood in Jordan 1989–94* (Washington, DC: The Washington Institute for Near East Policy, 1993).

Fox, Jonathan. 'Religion as an Overlooked Element in International Relations', *International Studies Review*, Vol. 3, No. 3, 2001, pp. 53–74.

Fuller, Graham. *Islamic Fundamentalism in the Northern Tier Countries* (Santa Monica, California: RAND, 1991).

Ghanayem, Ishaq and Voth, Alden. *The Kissinger Legacy: American Middle East Policy* (New York: Praeger, 1984).

Ghorayeb, Amal. *Hizbullah* (London: Pluto Press, 2000).

Gopin, Mark. *Between Eden and Armageddon: The Future of World Religions, Violence and Peacemaking* (Oxford: Oxford University Press, 2000).

Guazzone, Laura (ed.). *The Islamist Dilemma: The Political role of Islamist Movements in the Contemporary Arab World* (Reading: Ithaca Press, 1995).

Hal, John, Schuyler, Philip and Trinh, Sylvaine (eds.). *Apocalypse Observed: Religious Movements and Violence in North America, Europe, and Japan* (London: Routledge, 2000).

Halliday, Fred. *Islam and the Myth of Confrontation: Religion and Politics in the Middle East* (London: I.B. Tauris, 1995).

Heikal, Mohammed. *Secret Channels: The Inside Story of Arab-Israeli Peace Negotiations* (London: HarperCollins, 1996).

Hoffman, Bruce. *Recent Trends and Future Prospects of Iranian Sponsored International Terrorism* (Santa Monica, California: RAND, 1990).

Hourani, Hani, Awad, Taleb, Dabbas, Hamed and Kilani, Sa'eda. *Islamic Action Front Party* (Amman: Al-Urden Al-Jadid Research Center, 1993).

Hunter, Shireen. 'The Rise of Islamist Movements and the Western Response: Clash of Civilizations or Clash of Interests?', in Laura Guazzone (ed.). *The Islamist Dilemma: The Political role of Islamist Movements in the Contemporary Arab World* (Reading: Ithaca Press, 1995), pp. 316–50.

—— (ed.). *The Politics of Islamic Revivalism: Diversity and Unity* (Bloomington, Indiana: Indiana University Press, 1988).

Huntington, Samuel. 'The Clash of Civilizations?', *Foreign Affairs*, Vol. 72, No. 3, Summer 1993, pp. 19–23.

Indyk, Martin. 'The Implications for U.S. Policy', in Yehudah Mirsky and Ellen Rice (eds.). *Islam and the U.S. Challenges for the Nineties* (Washington, DC: The Washington Institute for Near East Policy, 1992), pp. 49–51.

Institute for National Strategic Studies. *Strategic Assessment 1995: U.S. Security Challenges in Transition* (Washington, DC: National Defense University Press, 1995).

Johansen, Robert. 'Radical Islam and Nonviolence: A Case Study of Religious Empowerment and Constraint among Pashtuns', *Journal of Conflict Resolution*, Vol. 34, No. 1, 1997, pp. 53–72.

Johnson, Chalmers. *Blowback: The Costs and Consequences of American Empire* (New York: Henry Holt and Company, 2001).

Johnston, Douglas and Sampson, Cynthia (eds.). *Religion: The Missing Dimension of Statecraft*. New York and Oxford: Oxford University Press, 1994.

Karam, Azza. *Women, Islamisms and the State: Contemporary Feminisms in Egypt* (London: Macmillan, 1998).

—— 'Islamisms: Globalisation, Religion and Power', in Ronaldo Munck and Purnaka L. de Silva (eds.). *Postmodern Insurgencies: Political Violence, Identity Formation and Peacemaking in Comparative Perspective* (London and New York: Macmillan and St. Martin's Press, 2000).

Kramer, Martin (ed.). *The Islamism Debate* (Tel Aviv: The Moshe Dayan Center for Middle Eastern and Islamic Studies, 1997).

LaFraniere, Sharon. 'Chechens Resigned to More Slaughter', *Guardian Weekly*, 14–20 November 2002, p. 32.

Lebor, Adam. *A Heart Turned East: Among the Muslims of Europe and America* (London: Warner Books, 1997).

Lewis, B. *What Went Wrong? Western Impact and Middle Eastern Response* (New York: Oxford University Press, 2001).

Milne, Seumas. 'Reasons to be Hated', *Guardian Weekly*, 28 November–4 December 2002, p. 13.

Mirsky, Yehudah and Rice, Ellen (eds.). *Islam and the U.S. Challenges for the Nineties* (Washington, DC: The Washington Institute for Near East Policy, 1992).

Nielsen, Jorgen. *Muslims in Western Europe* (Edinburgh: Edinburgh University Press, 1992).

Phillips, James. 'Rethinking U.S. Policy in the Middle East', *The Heritage Foundation Backgrounder*, No. 891, 10 April 1992, pp. 1–18.

Quandt, William B. 'Domestic Influences on United States Foreign Policy in the Middle East: The View from Washington', in Willard A. Belling (ed.).

The Middle East: Ten Years After Camp David (Washington: The Brookings
Institute, 1998), pp. 386–412.

Rashid, Ahmed. *Taliban: Militant Islam, Oil, and Fundamentalism in Central
Asia* (London: I.B. Tauris, 2000).

Robertson, R. *Globalization* (London: Sage, 1992).

Roy, Olivier. *Islam and Resistance in Afghanistan* (second edition) (Cambridge:
Cambridge University Press, 1990).

—— *The Failure of Political Islam* (London: I.B. Tauris, 1994).

—— *Afghanistan: From Holy War to Civil War* (Princeton: Princeton University
Press, 1995).

Rubin, Barry. *Radical Middle East States and U.S. Policy* (Washington, DC: The
Washington Institute for Near East Policy, 1993).

Samuel, Terence. 'The Peak of Political Power', *US News and World Report*, 23
December 2002, p. 42.

Schoenbaum, David. *The United States and the State of Israel* (Oxford: Oxford
University Press, 1993).

Sayyid, Bobby. *A Fundamental Fear: Eurocentrism and the Emergence of Islamism*
(London: Zed Books, 1997).

Smith, Christian (ed.). *Disruptive Religion: The Force of Faith in Social Movement
Activism* (London and New York: Routledge, 1996).

Stork, Joe. *Middle East Oil and Energy Crisis* (New York: Monthly Review Press,
1975).

Taheri, Emir. *Nest of Spies: America's Journey to Disaster in Iran* (London:
Hutchinson, 1988).

Telham, Shibli. *Power and Leadership in International Bargaining: The Path to
the Camp David Accords* (New York: Columbia University Press, 1990).

*The BBC Reports: On America, Its Allies and Enemies, and the Counterattack on
Terrorism* (with an Introduction by Harold Evans) (Woodstock and New
York: The Overlook Press, 2001).

Tillman, Seth. *The United States in the Middle East. Interests and Obstacles*
(Bloomington, Indiana: Indiana University Press, 1982).

Vertovec, S. and Peach, C. (eds.). *Islam in Europe: The Politics of Islam and
Community* (London: Macmillan, 1997).

Waters, Malcolm. *Globalization* (London and New York: Routledge, 1995).

Wilner, John and Bloementhal, Dan (eds.) *America and the Middle East: An
Enduring Role in a Changing World* (Washington, DC: The Washington
Institute for Near East Policy, 1995).

Newspapers and Magazines

Al-Ahram (Arabic)
Al-Ahram Weekly
Al-Hayat (Arabic)
The Economist
Guardian Weekly
Le Monde Diplomatique
New York Times
US News and World Report

2

Restructuring Political Islam: Transnational Belonging and Muslims in France and Germany

Valérie Amiraux

Introduction

> The Muslim encounter with the 'West' is an on-going drama that has intertwined the histories of the two peoples for over fourteen centuries. (Haddad, 1998)

The respective and mutual shaping of memories from both the Islamic world and the western hemisphere is embedded in a complex and violent history structured mainly around conflicts. This does not mean that collaboration and common interests never occurr. During the last three decades of the twentieth century, European Islam (the Muslims living in Europe stemming from the migrants settled in various European countries after the 1960s) became an important feature of the relationship between Islam in the countries of origin (mainly from the Middle East – including Turkey – and North Africa) and Islam in the western world. This peculiar role of European Islam is based on a simultaneous evolution: for western contexts, it meant dealing more and more with Muslim citizens, whereas in Muslim communities, it meant coping with the problem of living in a non-Islamic environment as a minority and having to answer to radically new and challenging questions, in particular concerning the issue of authority. This chapter offers a reflection on this parallel evolution and puts a special emphasis on the role played by political Islam in this picture.[1]

Islam can now be legitimately considered as established more than 'transplanted' in most of the western European countries (Dassetto and Bastenier, 1993; Dassetto, 1996). Indeed, a new phase began after the 1970s with increased concentration on the needs of younger (second- and third-generation) Muslims. The dynamics that evolved were linked with the settlement in Europe of new types of believers: those who were young, born (or educated) in Europe, some of whom were citizens of the countries of residence and involved socially and politically in ways that differed from their parents. In terms of the organization of religious life, this change resulted in a growing visibility of Islamic features in the cities (such as mosques and veils), and in the emergence of requests for legal and institutional recognition. For local authorities, this institutionalization process means identifying a single, representative partner for negotiation. Despite this common evolution (summarized below) Islam in Europe remains extremely differentiated from one country to the other, largely depending on the countries of origin of these Muslims, but also on the judicial and political configuration of the various local and national contexts they inhabit.[2] To be a Muslim in Europe no longer means seeking to reproduce the conditions of practice of faith based on experiences in the country of origin.

European Muslims claim certain rights, including the recognition of their religious specificity, with a particular emphasis on issues such as education, workers' rights, legal status and in some case financial advantages. These global changes in the relationship between individuals and faith – and thereby even with community (i.e. effects on the significance of membership to a group) – do not mean, however, the disappearance of the link with the Muslim countries at large and with the society of origin in particular. Rather, it signifies an increasing complexity. Intensification of communication, the increasing role played by the media, the transnational movement of people, ideas and money from one territory to another, all indicate it would be a mistake to assume that the development of European Islam is disconnected from religious agendas in Muslim countries.[3] Several questions arise about the installation, operation and mobilization of resources by these actors, characterized by a capacity to function in networks (Amiraux, 1999).

European countries may have felt this kind of double bind more strongly since September 11, 2001, between an insider and outsider Islam.[4] The connection between Islam in Europe and the terrorist attacks in the United States has been immediate and implicit even if 'Muslim organisations were quick and explicit in their condemnation of the New York and Washington attacks' in the words of Jorgen Nielsen (2002), referring to Britain.[5] Many discourses haven been produced and projected on September 11. The inability, some months later, to produce a satisfactory narrative and explanation concerning the meaning of such a spectacular event – organized by a tremendously effective bureaucracy and performed by committed individuals who consciously opted to sacrifice themselves – may be related to a set of unanswered questions. First, a question of analysis: should the focus be on institutions, policy-makers and public opinion, or should it be on religious aspects, rituals, traditions, texts or individual commitment to a community? The second question concerns the unit of observation: the national contexts, countries of origin or host countries, federations, associations, individuals and official groups. The last question comes back to the issue of definition. Which one would be the most relevant? Whose political Islam/terrorism/fundamentalism are we speaking about? In the end, all three sets of questions can be subsumed in a single one. Do we know whom we are talking about?

In this chapter, I propose to review the various places and degrees of interaction inside what I designate as a 'transnational space', on the basis of examples focusing mainly on two contexts, Germany and France. The concept of transnational space enables a reflection on the dramatic political and journalistic portrayals, whereby there is often an automatic identification between Islam and a potential internal threat.[6] More than crossing borders or representing a bilateral link, a transnational space connects the specific practices of networks with other features, so that the space in which a citizen is allowed to participate politically is not necessarily always her/his place of residence. It also means identifying the multiple types of agencies intervening (or at least trying to) in the political discussion over the management of Islam in the country of settlement, and the forms, structures, various functions and sets of actors interacting in addition to the exclusive state framework.

The Changing Face of Islam in Europe: Belonging to a Larger *Umma*?

Islam is the second largest religion in the European Union if we consider statistics identifying Muslims according to their ethnic origin.[7] However, this population does not appear as homogeneous, unified and equally engaged with a religious identity.

In fact, the two real trends which are working among the European Muslims are: firstly, a vocal fundamentalist school of thought, trying to build a reconstructed community by preaching individuals, and addressing the real concerns of individuals who lost most of their community link; and secondly, the silent majority of the believers, who found their way on the basis of compromises, adaptations, and makeshift ideology. (Roy, 2000: 1)

Speaking of a Muslim community would therefore be a clear misinterpretation of a complex reality. Just as there are ways of being a Muslim in Europe (Khosrokhavar, 1997; Cesari, 1998; Roy, 1999), so there are different ways of looking at the relationship between the Muslim populations settled in Europe and their environment (which is also neither coherent nor homogeneous).[8] The political and legal frameworks of dealing with Islam by public agencies also differ considerably within the European Union (Ferrari and Bradney, 2000). The distinction between nationalities, on the other hand, is easier to make. While in France most of the Muslims come from the Maghreb (North Africa: Algeria, Morocco and Tunisia), in Germany 70 per cent are of Turkish origin, followed by natives of Bosnia-Herzegovina.[9] The distribution in Germany follows patterns according to a market logic (job demand), but also submits to the principle of distribution (*Gleichverteilung*) imposed by the regions welcoming the refugees, and implemented since 1992 in the employment areas of the Ruhr (where there is a concentration of Turkish people constituting the highest percentage of foreigners).[10]

Thus, while the activities of the Turkish Islamic associations are distributed between Cologne and Berlin, those of the Bosnians and Albanians of Kosovo are largely located in the Bade Wurtemberg.[11] In socio-economic terms, profiling the Muslim populations is almost as difficult as counting them. Economically less and less excluded, their professional activities are diverse, particularly in the context of a dynamic business ethic combining high levels of education and political commitment.[12] Finally, a common feature of Islam in France and Germany is the clear identification of religion with a personal and individual choice (Roy, 1999; Amiraux, 2001). The diversification of religious practices (Khosrokhavar, 1997) appears in a context where Muslims are living as a minority in a secularized Europe and where religion is more or less neutralized in terms of its social influence and normative value in the public sphere. For Muslims, expressing an attachment to a religious faith becomes an individual experience before being a collective one.

This evolution has been studied by various scholars. During the last two decades, the literature on Islam in Europe has developed considerably. The growing political interest in Muslim social realities encompasses two dimensions. In countries such as Spain and Italy, where the presence of Islam linked to immigrant guestworkers is more recent than in 'traditional host countries' (such as France, Germany and Great Britain), social scientists have produced a wealth of information (Moreras, 1999; Allievi and Dassetto 1993; Saint-Blancat, 1999), about both local contexts and broader regional dynamics (Dassetto et al., 2001).

On the other hand, the contemporary generation of experts on Islam in Europe is more and more emancipated from their 'forefathers', being either specialists on the Middle East who converted their knowledge to the field of European Islam or Orientalists. These two movements are particularly apparent if one surveys the growing number of edited volumes under the umbrella term 'European Islams' (see, for instance, Gerholm and Lithman, 1988; Nonneman et al., 1996; Vertovec and Peach, 1997; Shadid and Van Koningsveld, 1991, 1996).

The convergence of these two kinds of analysis helped produce a shift in the focus of studies on Islam, in terms of both the object of the study as well as the theoretical frameworks used. While the first publications on Islam in France, Germany, Belgium, the Netherlands and Great Britain usually consisted predominantly of descriptions of the organizational and associative dimensions of Muslim social life (Kepel, 1987; Schiffauer, 1987, 1991; Binswanger, 1988; Kepel and Leveau, 1988; Lewis, 1994; Heitmeyer, 1997 Rath et al., 1997;), and of an analysis of the movement towards an institutionalization of Islam (Landman, 1992; Dassetto et al., 2001), it seems that more recently an attempt is being made to focus on the growing heterogeneity of Muslims living in Europe.[13] This includes an emphasis on new issues, such as the relationships between individuals and their 'community of belonging' (Khosrokhavar, 1997; Cesari, 1998), the growing significance of gender aspects and mysticism (Amiraux, 2001; Jonker and Sakaranaho, 2003), and more recently the need for an analysis of new forms of authority and leadership for Muslims in Europe (Allievi, 1998; Fregosi 1998).

It is precisely this non-homogeneity of Muslims in Europe, increasingly witnessed by specialists, which should prevent confusion between Islamic activism/militancy (elsewhere called Islamism or political Islam) and Islamic associations aiming at improving the living conditions of these Muslims.[14] Rather, this heterogeneity invites one to explore the distinctions within the same community of believers. What makes some Muslims decide to engage in violence and terrorism while others select more inclusive types of activities? How can we explain the success in Europe of movements which have been either ignored or unsuccessful in the Middle East?[15] The notion of community (*Umma*) seems to be central in explaining these questions (Mandaville, 2001). Mandaville proposes the hypothesis of 'translocal politics', defined as new forms of politics emerging from the Muslim world's experience of globalization. In his conception, the transnational (also called translocal) 'is a space in which new forms of post-ethnic and post-national identities are constituted and not simply one in which prior identities assert themselves' (Mandaville, 2001: 46).

Assuming the transnational/translocal dimension of mobilization among Muslims and Islamic organizations in Europe means identifying two features: the regular interactions between agents and the participation of at least one non-nation state actor (Risse-Kappen, 1995). The impact of these networks of non-state actors on the diffusion of information, ideas and values from one territory to another is central. However, it remains difficult to evaluate accurately their impact on policy-making. Risse-Kappen explains the importance of two sets of structures in his evaluation of the transnational actor's capacity for action: the domestic structures (meaning the normative arrangement which constitutes the state and the society, institutional features and their link to politics such as the idea of citizenship and the relationship between central and local governments), the degree of institutionalization of the core issue at the international level (Risse-Kappen, 1995). In sum, the more a state is fragmented, the more civil society is organized, and the easier it is for transnational actors to affect international and national politics. It would therefore be mistaken to reduce the associative networks of Islamic organizations in Europe to a simple reproduction and importation of political and religious projects 'made in' the Middle East. Rather, what should be underlined is that the way Muslim populations and organizations develop in Europe is primarily a function of the local and national contexts of settlement, particularly at the legal level.

The changing face of Islam in Europe therefore has many features and theological implications: is Europe *dar al-harb, dar al-Islam* or *dar al-shahada*?[16] If Islam is becoming primarily an individual issue (a code of behaviour) rather than a social and collective one, how could it negotiate a position in a legal context despite a nonsymmetrical relationship with western frameworks? Consequently, to whom should authority over the 'community of believers' be given? It should not be forgotten that the growing demand for the institutionalization of their faith by Muslim migrants in Europe (through requests for more visibility for religious infrastructures) parallels the rising politicization of religious claims in Muslim countries. This coincidence gives more substance to the hypothesis of the relevance of transnational politics and mobilization to Islam in Europe. On the one hand, the main traditional sponsors of Islamic organizations (Saudi Arabia, Libya and Pakistan) found alternative channels for their worldwide strategies of promoting Islamic interests (mainly expressed through their interest in sponsoring education and places of worship) in Europe. On the other hand, getting more visible and representative as legitimate partners of public institutions in the West may also have strengthened the roles that Muslims can play in their countries of origin.

Using the Legal Resources in European Countries

Laws of association are the only frameworks in which Muslims can express their cultural and religious claims in France as well as in Germany. The problem of Islam in Europe goes beyond the conflict between regimes of private laws, 'placing the question of European Islam within a private international law framework underlines it as a question concerning primarily foreigners' (Ferrari and Bradney, 2000: 7). Legal national contexts affect the interaction between Islam as a religion and the various European states differently. The constitutional separation in France between state and religion, effective since December 1905, is currently a central pillar of the republican identity claimed by most politicians. As article 2 of this law expresses it: 'the state does not recognize nor subsidize any religion, thus sustaining the equal treatment of different religions'. The law on association (July 1901) 'acknowledges freedom of association to be a fundamental public freedom' (Basdevant-Gaudemet, 2000: 99).[17]

The German context also provides for particular organizational requirements for any type of religious associations – not only Islamic ones. Religious freedom is a fundamental constitutional and individual right for everybody living in Germany. The use of one or other resource is also connected to the emergence of what Rokkan (1970) designates as traditional alliances in the political arena and distinguishing between four traditional ones – periphery-centre, religious, urban-rural, workers and bourgeois class – regardless of degrees of institutionalization. In Germany, religious cleavage is institutionalized and pacified, thus leaving more space for this kind of mobilization. This pacification of religious conflict itself comes into play in the relationship between state and church as defined by the Constitution of Weimar of 1919 (WRV), now partly integrated into the *Grundgesetz* (Fundamental Law, hereafter GG) as article 140. Three main principles determine the relation between church and state. The first underlines the absence of a state church. The principle of separation establishes the reciprocal independence of the two actors, affirming official neutrality: the state is prohibited from intervening in the church's sphere of activity and that of other religious communities. No organizational link connects the church to the state, while a principle of cooperation prevails, based on the distinction of the respective duties (*Aufgabengebiete*) and the separation of both spheres (Maunz et al., 1994). The relations between church and state are founded on neither fusion nor dependence, but on cooperation. It is not a question of a 'heinous separation between religious communities and State. On the contrary, certain material bases as the freedom of activity are guaranteed to the religious communities found useful by the State' (Walter, 1989: 194). The second main principle concerns the neutrality of the state, that is, its non-identification with any religion in particular, as well as freedom of religion for all citizens, parity[18] and neutrality at the ethical level (the neutrality of officials vis-à-vis all citizens in any administrative procedures). The third and last is the right to self-determination, or free will, for the religious communities (*die Selbstbestimmungsrecht der Religionsgemeinschaften*).[19] Therefore, 'the German system of civil ecclesiastical law is based on three fundamental principles: neutrality, tolerance and parity' (Robbers, 2000: 150).

All Islamic associations are recorded officially and work within a legal framework of the common rights associations (*eingetragene Vereine*). They are not supposed to threaten either the internal or external security of the state. The separation from the governments of their respective countries of origin is crucial: it facilitates autonomy for the Islamic associations around sensitive matters, as in the management of religious staff, such as imams and religious instructors, traditionally managed by the state in Turkey, for instance.[20]

Turkish Realities

Historically, Islam was considered potentially threatening to the path of modernization chosen by the secular nationalist Turkish leader, Kemal Atatürk. Hence, any Islamic entity was strictly excluded from the public space and controlled by the state. Stigmatization and prohibition, however, never succeeded in weakening the intensity of religious feelings and consolidation of some organizations, in particular the religious brotherhoods. Comparing the German and Turkish contexts helps in understanding the nature of this initial 'trauma' and the opportunity represented by the settlement of about two million Turks in Germany. Turkish Islam in Germany is structured by a legal framework which allows 'exported' Turkish Islamic groups to organize or reconstitute themselves as associations.

Schematically, the Turkish associations can be divided into two categories. The first is where the organization uses Germany as an operational base in exile. This includes most of the political groups and parties of religious inspiration, which, for economic reasons connected with the internal development of the country of origin, are unable to pursue their objectives. The second category involves those aiming for Turkish integration in Germany: workers' groups, associations of immigrants, parents, doctors, and so on. Groups concerned with Islam formally focus on collating cultural data (habits, values, symbols and rituals) which are considered defining characteristics of the identity of believers. To some extent, this relative freedom of organization facilitates the construction of autonomous spaces and decisions away from official or state control, and is exclusively based on community-type affiliation.

The major Turkish federations appeared in Germany at the beginning of the 1980s, aiming to present a single, unified counterpart to negotiate with the state, and also attempting to subscribe to the legal requirements within the statute of public law corporation (*Körperschaft des öffentlichen Rechts*). In the language of public law, corporations designate the associations which, to achieve common duties, function according to a system of alliances and undertake social work.[21]

Bosnian Realities

To some extent, the settlement of Bosnian Islamic groups in Germany shares the chronology of the Turkish ones. Arriving in

Germany during the 1960s, the first religious organizations appeared at the end of the 1970s. The IGMG[22]-AK, on the one hand, the Federation of Islamic Communities (SDA), on the other, each occupies an equivalent position in the religious field, and mobilizes similar tools. In 1994, the Bosnian *dzemat* (groups) amalgamated into the Federation of the Islamic Community (*Vereinigung Islamischer Gemeinden der Bosniaken in Deutschland*, VIGB), satellites of the Islamska Zadjenica (Islamic Community, the organisation of Alija Izetbegovic since 1969) which until then had expressed very limited interest in the diaspora.[23]

There are many similarities in approach between the Turkish Islamic groups and Bosnian ones, offering language courses for children and adults (often with the local authorities' support), TV channels, magazines and the distribution of newspapers from the country of origin.[24] The Bosnians are quite militant about the recognition of their language in Germany (it is officially recognized only in Austria) and advocate for this in their newsletter (*Liljan*).

There are certain nuances, however, which effectively distinguish the actions of both actors. Whereas the SDA (Stranska Demokratia Aktia/Community of Democratic Action, the largest organization of Bosnians in the Federal Republic) effectively monopolizes the management of Islam and of the Bosnian diaspora (particularly since 1994 by taking control of the consulates – local managers brought together by regions – and of financial resources such as taxes), Islamic Turkish associations are still in competition with each other. In 1984, for example, Cemalettin Kaplan broke away from AMGT to organize an independent group based in Stuttgart, the Federation der islamischen Gemeinden Gemeinschaften (ICCB) and automatically declared itself the Caliphate of the Islamic state of Turkey in exile. Similar attempts to gain autonomy have been experienced in Stuttgart and Frankfurt by some Bosnian mosques withdrawing from the SDA umbrella. However, the separatist inclinations of some independent imams are being curbed by immediate financial difficulties.

Being a Muslim in Europe remains more of an individual choice than the result of a particular coercive experience. Secularization, acculturation or the use of one concept at the expense of another, is not enough to convey the reality of this tension between individual performance and membership of a group. These dichotomies (individual/group, cultural/political) are maintained by transnational dynamics and characterize the operating mode of the associations.

The distinction between policy and culture is thereafter assumed by the individual–community dialectic which fashions the Islam 'produced' in Europe (Ghalioun, 1997). In the case of Bosnian Islamic groups, this division between cultural Islam and political Islam is manifested in a clear rupture that occurred in 1990. This distinguished between the pre-war and post-war period, and is visible in the way that groups organize. The SDA began to establish its own network within the community through a cultural society, 'Preporod' (Renaissance), the humanitarian/welfare organization 'Merhamet' and other youth associations, allowing the mobilization of interests and support in times of crisis or elections, without losing touch with the young Muslims of Europe. In the case of AK and of AMGT, this separation of the political and cultural projects is apparent in the transformation of the AMGT into two organizations during the Conference of 3 June 1995 in Frankfurt: the Islamische Gesellschaft Milli Gorus (IGMG) (dedicated to political and social work) and the Europaische Moscheebau– und Unterstützungs Gemeinschaft (EMUG), which manages finance and real estate.

The process of establishment follows a similar chronology in all the cases in France and Germany, even going as far as confirming the implementation of identical protection and mobility methods (e.g. the change of name). All the actors involved in political activities in the name of religious organizations arrived in Germany with an experience of political opposition and know-how in terms of the use of religion as an instrument of organization and mobilization, based on symbolic repertoires connected with an individual experience of the policy.[25] The concept of 'repertoire' developed by Tilly is connected with the time and place in which all types of organized movements are evolving. This repertoire changes with the political developments inside the country of origin and serves the achievement of goals that cannot be pursued directly (Cohen, 1997). It is then capable of changing in relation to a crisis context (such as war), but also imitating by interaction with other groups in the formal migratory space in Germany the use of associations to organise the action.

With this in mind, the common cultural denominators act as a toolbox, composed of rituals, symbols, histories and visions of the world used to build action strategies. The capacity of organizations built on the basis of the religious reference is moreover directly connected with the population's cultural distinctiveness (the conscience of belonging to the same group and loyalty binds), its social homogeneity and its political position. The more the group is incorporated internally, the stronger and wider is its capacity to organize and mobilize.

In the German context, it is also important to link the relative *laissez-faire* towards religious organizations with, on the one hand, the very restricted policy of naturalization, (Soysal, 1994; Guiraudon, 2000) and, on the other, with the very specific nature of the German state as semi-sovereign (Katzenstein, 1987). Further, until the beginning of the 1990s, Chancellor Kohl's Administration, and in particular its Foreign Affairs Minister Klaus Kinkel, considered Islam above all as part of its foreign policy agenda.

As for France's public management of Islam, the colonial past served the creation of a Muslim exception to *laïcité* (secularism) (Fregosi, 1998). Following the 'colonial path' in which the French state was administering religious affairs (control over teaching, preaching, and so on), the public management of contemporary Islam is based on a 'top-down' logic aimed at identifying (or even creating) allies among the Muslim populations settled on French soil.[26]

Several steps can be discerned about the way public authorities tried to help the creation of an institutionalized Islam and a representative structure. Successive Ministers of Interior (Joxe in 1989, Pasqua in 1994, Chevènement in 2000) have played a role in this. The *Conseil d'Orientation et de Réflexion sur l'Islam en France* (CORIF – the Council of Orientation and Reflection on Islam in France), in March 1989, represented the first concrete attempt to create a mediation committee for consultation on concrete matters with French public institutions. By the mid-1990s (1994–95) and following the influence of Charles Pasqua, the emphasis was on finding a single partner (essentially wanting it to be the Paris mosque). From this initiative emerged the Charte du culte musulman en France (Charter of Muslim Cults in France), another attempt to establish nationally legal parameters for Islam in France. The former and still ongoing process follows the initiative of Jean Pierre Chevènement to launch a national consultation on Islam in France (Consultation sur l'islam de France), initiated in October 1999 by a letter sent by the minister to invite Muslim organizations, and influential Muslim personalities, to sign a common document summarizing the basic legal principles organizing the relationship between public agencies and sects in France. This last initiative is now entering its final phase whereby mosques are organizing elections of Islamic representatives across France.[27]

These state initiatives are not systematically approved by all religious leaders, since here again (as in Germany) competition remains fierce between the potential applicants to the position of official partner of the State (such as the Fédération nationale des musulmans de France and the Union des organisations Islamiques de France, to name but two). In the case of the most recent French state project (Consultation), some popular local leaders accused the French government of promoting the interests of radical groups (such as *tabligh* and Muslim brotherhood) considering them as legitimate potential partners for discussion, despite the fact that they refuse to re-evaluate their interpretations of the religious texts in light of contemporary contexts. A clear distinction has to be made between a strict administrative view on how to manage Islam (meaning the state hesitating between a clear intervention and a *laissez-faire* policy) and the daily attitude towards Islam on a practical basis.[28] Several conflicts have regularly emerged around practical questions. Places for Muslims in cemeteries, holidays, veils in school, animal slaughtering, opening of places of worship, representation of Islam in public establishments and issues of personal legal status (especially concerning marriage) are among the main ones discussed in France as well as in Germany. In both countries, the solutions to these discussions are increasingly sorted out locally.

Mosques still represent very sensitive issues in terms of religious, cultural but also political visibility and questions of funding.[29] This is captured in the question posed by a journalist in 1996: '*Prayer rooms or offices for political parties?*'[30] Mosques express an authority, assure visibility aimed at a local audience and therefore contribute to the competition (especially in view of their size, minaret and cupola) between organizations in their fight for recognition in the host country. Often very simple places (such as backyards) the mosque is also useful for collecting funds, organizing elections and serving as a place of registration for electoral polls. For the SDA, mosques function as a relay, sorting the voters and enabling subsidiary organizations like Merhamet or Preporod to benefit from their social centrality.

Imams and religious educators also represent very sensitive issues especially in terms of training – such as whether they have to be trained in Europe or 'imported' from the countries of origin. Their status remains equivocal in either case.[31]

Faced with these pragmatic questions regarding the religious management of the various Muslims populations in Europe, and recognizing the financial and political connections with Islamic countries, the radicalization of Islam falls within the domain of a minority of groups or individuals, such as the Algerian Islamist ideologue Rashid Ghanouchi (in Great Britain) and some ex-members of the Islamic Front in Germany. Also in Germany, the case of Cemalettin Kaplan as a self-declared revolutionary or radical is unique. Described by Schiffauer (2000) as the most radical group settled in Germany which was inspired by the Iranian revolutionary movement, and aiming at restoring the Caliphate, it has been banned since 12 December 2002 by the German government after its speaker admitted having met Bin Laden in 1996.

However, the confusion between radical and moderate components of political Islam still dominates public perception of Islam in Europe. The perception of Islam through a security lens is directly responsible for the manner in which Muslims in Europe are seen as a potential Islamic danger. In France, for example, since 1995 there have been regular incursions by the Ministry of Interior (Burgat, 1995).

Symbolic violence may be an interpretation of the shift from passive to active expression of forms of belonging. Bigo (2001) points out that this designation of Islam as a potential internal enemy should be linked to the broader evolution in which internal and external security (traditionally two separate domains that were essentially the concern of different institutions, police and army) now appear to be converging regarding border, order and the possible threats to identity, linked to (im)migration (Bigo, 2001: 91).

Islam belongs to the set of threats that transgresses national identities and territories. Using the metaphor of the Möbius strip, Bigo explains how the merging of internal and external security is a reflection of 'the lowering of the level of acceptability of the other' rather than a consequence of an objective increase of threats in the contemporary epoch (2001: 111). Moreover, 'internal and external security are embedded in the figure of the "enemy within", or of the outsider inside, which is increasingly labelled with the catchword "immigrant", who is, depending on the context and the political interests, a foreigner or a national citizen representing a minority' (2001: 112). Moving from one place to another, and bringing with them cultural and religious diversity, Muslim migrants blur borders and promote a deterritorialized Islam. The transnational dimension of this is more explicitly visible during national crises occurring in the countries of origin.

Transnational: From Empirical Observation to Theory

Transnational indicates a circulation between multiple political spaces, without a limited, unique and exclusive cultural or political membership. There are as many avenues for transnational mobilization as there are levels of networks and various types of actors. The last section of this chapter examines two dimensions: how, in times of crisis, transnational dynamics emerge as resources to escape specific national settings in a limited time frame; and yet, how the Salman Rushdie affair failed in demonstrating the existence of a transnational community among Muslims in the United Kingdom.

Several political events illustrate the existence of transnational links deriving from the interconnectedness of at least two national spaces and territories. The practices are based on the capacity of actors, individually as well as collectively, to use and convert resources from one national space to the other. The so-called 'crisis of the Balkans', starting with the conflict in the former Yugoslavia in 1991 and ending with the signing of a military agreement between NATO and the Federal Republic of Yugoslavia, and the United Nations Resolution (June 1999) putting an end to the war in Kosovo, all provide the means of observing the activation of solidarity networks, particularly in Germany.

During this period, Muslim populations have been perceived as both victims and actors able to enter politics and organise the representation of their interests. Some political parties have emerged, making a choice on whether or not to express publicly their Islamic character, for example in their names (Bougarel and Clayer, 2001: esp. 9–75). In a way, this crisis created new links with other Islamic countries (Turkey), helped the partial re-Islamization of some national identities and even facilitated the integration of the Muslims from the Balkans into the core of the Muslim community.

Beyond the geographical proximity of Germany to the conflict areas of the former Yugoslavia, the relative flexibility of its legal mechanisms regarding political asylum made it a focus for refugees. This specific 'crisis' influx is added to a local (mainly Turkish) Muslim population living in Germany since 1961.[32]

The Turkish Islamic associative network was, at the beginning of the 1990s, quite well established and provided their Balkan brothers with the logistic and moral support they were looking for. The role played by some Turkish Islamic groups, and in particular by the unofficial representative association in Europe of the AK Partisi, is in this respect exemplary. Just as they did when Algerians from the Front Islamique du Salut (FIS) were leaving Algeria in 1994–95, the infrastructures of the AMGT (Vereinigung der Neuen Weltsicht in Europa/Avrupa Milli Gorus Teskilatlari),[33] in particular in the south of Germany, served as an essential support for some of the political groups coming from the Balkans, and in particular from Bosnia. This collaboration mainly takes the form of providing material support (places of worship, allocation of seats in local associations, computing services, and so on) and financial help (specifically fundraising).

The German security agencies (primarily the BVS – Bundesverfassungschutz) highlight the greater attention they pay to these methods of organization and of mobilization at the financial and political levels.[34] The Kosovar Albanians are presented as the most active militants, particularly in the south of Germany. In a 1997 report, the LPK (a Kosovar Albanian organization) is identified as one of the 'foreign political tendencies' and classified as the most threatening to national security. Thus, in spite of a slight fall in terms of membership numbers each year, the Islamic organizations remain the most important ones in terms of their potential, with IGMG (ex-AMGT) topping the list. Since 1993, the AMGT and its 26,200 members have been among the strongest of the foreign extremist associations declared a threat to national security.

The report of the BVS on the German capital, Berlin, reproduces the same classification.[35] The reasons given by the BVS for their monitoring of the association are two-fold: it aspires to a state based on the Qur'an; and religion and policy are given the same importance, which, the report notes, has negative consequences for 'democracy and the people'. The report also underlies the AMGT's expressed endeavours to present a moderate image, which is disputed by the anti-Semitic sentiments expressed publicly by some leaders. The monitored associations are considered in the annual reports to be a threat to federal security. It is also clearly stated that Turkish Islamic associations are active in supporting other Muslim organizations from Bosnia and from Algeria (such as Front Islamique du Salut, or FIS). In fact, members of the FIS took part in meetings of these organizations in which the topic of Algeria was broached.

The groups from the former Yugoslavia are not quoted in the 1997 BVS report at the federal level, but are, on the other hand, noted in the regional report of the Bade-Würtemberg (Land) where 317,525 citizens of the former Yugoslavia are registered and described as 'not dangerous'.[36] The number of potentially violent individuals is considered to be between 100 and 180 people in the 1997 Land report, which stressed the absence of intra-community rivalry among Bosnians. Since September 11, 2001, the restrictions of German policy (in terms of national security and of border controls for migration) have directly affected some of the negotiations between local authorities and Islamic associations. This is especially evident around matters of religious education and teaching, whereby the transnational connections of some of the Islamic groups settled in Germany are at the core of the concerns raised by the local authorities.

The professionalization of the Islamic organizations and the capacity of their leaders to mobilize are evident during moments of crisis (war and conflicts) or of successes in the country of origin. The electoral success of the Refah Partisi (today, AK Partisi), the Turkish Islamist party directed at that time by Necmettin Erbakan, the subsequent end of the Akyol coalition government (July 1996–June 1997) and the conflict in the former Yugoslavia, to some extent have acted as catalysts for mobilization in the territories of migration. Although each incident is different (electoral victory on one hand, ethnic conflict on the other), 'triggering events' or 'suddenly imposed grievances' serve to mobilize Islamic associations in Europe.

The maintenance of links, interests and emotions connected with the country of origin are maintained through different types of events. Regular visits of central and influential personalities (prime ministers, ministers and prominent intellectual figures) are one means of maintaining and reviving such linkages.

The connection between the activation of transnational networks and important or unexpected events of domestic or international policy is immediate, and not only as far as religious movements are concerned.[37] In this respect, the stability of the German political context compensates for the fluctuations of circumstances in the countries of origin. The Bosnian cause played a key role in the organizing and distribution of humanitarian aid from 1992, in turn leading to solidarity networks which could henceforth be redeployed during the conflict in Kosovo. The transnational connections were also used by the Turks, like the Bosnians, between 1992 and 1995, in orchestrating an imagined *Umma* (Roy, 1996; Khosrokhavar, 1997).[38]

In fact, it is at the financial level that the working methods and objectives of the various associations appear to be the most illustrative of a transnational dynamic, which is multidimensional.

First, there are the main sponsoring and internationally reputable institutions, which are also active in the European space, such as Al Rabita. Since 1962, in particular through its European section in Brussels, Al Rabita has had as its objective defending Islamic minorities in non-Muslim countries. It also manages the issue of the construction of mosques all over the world, either as a central agent (as in the case of the central mosque in Rome) or as an intermediary (supporting specific projects with the participation of other states, such as Mantes La Jolie in France). Also created by Saudi Arabia, the Organization of the Islamic Conference (OIC) is the second most important institution for fundraising, mainly through the intermediary of the Islamic Development Bank (since 1973). Parallel to these institutions, some private banks also became central in activities sponsoring European Islam, as do NGOs such as the International Islamic Relief Organisation (IIRO) and the Islamic Relief Agency (Bellion Jourdan, 2001).

Second, sponsorship and fundraising are linked with the *halal* business. The leaders' identities make it possible to draw the contours of financial nebulae in this domain. In the case of AMGT-IGMG in 1994–95, the Selam GMBH was the central organization for the *halal* business (a sixth of food trade on German soil would be in the hands of the AMGT). Selam Video and Hicret Verlag (for pilgrimages) are other financial sources dealing with the non-alimentary sectors (*Süddeutsche Zeitung*, 28 April 1995).

In addition, taxation is an essential resource exploited by various types of agencies – mainly but not exclusively state taxes. In 1993, the Bosnian government taxed 10 per cent of all the incomes of its community based in Germany. In 1994–95, about DM 7 million was raised through these optional contributions. In July 1998, a journalist working for the *Frankfurter Allgemeine Zeitung* uncovered similar financial networks collecting funds among the Kosovar in Germany for the KLA army, contributing to strengthening the opposition to the Serbs. The methods used for collecting money are very similar from one organization to another, and nationality is not relevant in this respect. Whether in cash, by cheque or money transfer, fundraising takes place in or in front of the mosque, or during association meetings, and is often publicized in community journals (such as *The Voice of Kosovo, Liljan, AMGT bülten*, and so on). In the specific case of the Kosovars abroad, fundraising has been more centralized since 1992 (i.e. following the declaration of an independent Republic). As in the Bosnian case, the Fund of the

Republic of Kosovo was made up of monthly levies (3 per cent) on income and was placed under Bujar Bukoshi's (a leading figure among Kosovar diaspora) control, assigning it officially to schools, hospitals, crèches, hospices and orphanages. As of March 1998 strong internal dissensions regarding the management and real assignment of the money raised emerged: should it be distributed to violent or non-violent actors engaged in the conflict in Kosovo? The Serb offensive accelerated the fundraising organized by one group in particular (Die Heimat ruft; literally, 'the fatherland calls'), the money being mainly devoted to the purchase of equipment (vehicles, weapons), food supplies and direct support. Since 27 July 1998, several people responsible for the foundation Die Heimat ruft have been accused of participating in a criminal organization and the association's bank account has been frozen.[39]

In short, as long as a group of immigrants is settled and organized, the interaction with events taking place in the country of origin will have a direct and immediate translation abroad.

The Rushdie affair is a good illustration of the complexity of the transnational modes of belonging (Blom, 1999). It also shows the ambiguity and inconsistency of the concept of *Umma*, often used to denote a transnational community of Muslims. As Blom points out, 'this kind of approach and perception was strongly revived during the Rushdie Affair' (Blom, 1999: 193). Transnational modes cover many dimensions: the way the event was presented as echoing what was happening in Iran and the way public opinion in Rushdie's continental Europe feared the contagion from crossing the Channel. Between September 1988 and January 1989, the role played by the United Kingdom Islamic Mission, the followers of Mawdudi from India and Pakistan and the Saudi networks of fundraisers was significant in the first phase of the anti-Rushdie protest. In the second phase, the Deobandi and Barelvi associations developed a kind of counter-diplomatic strategy oriented towards mass mobilization (Kepel, 2000: 288–90). Finally, the anti-Rushdie protest became an international campaign, perceived as a popular mobilization against a terrorist threat (Kepel, 2000).

In this short chronology, it needs to be said that Khomeini's fatwa was pronounced in February 1989, at the end of these three phases of mobilization. As Kepel points out, what is extremely puzzling is the convergence of condemnation by three different types of actors (Iranian, Indo-Pakistanis and Muslim brothers) and the way the Iranian fatwa affected the position of European Islam as a whole. In the same way as the Iranian revolution of 1979 was a catalyst in the shifting European public perception of Islam (from Islam as a factor of social peace, to Islam as an international threat with roots in Europe), Khomeini's fatwa against Rushdie confirmed the previously vague suspicion in European public perception that Muslims were more loyal to their respective countries of origin.

This mobilization was transnational in the sense that it went beyond national borders, but was also a function of the particular context of competition between Islamic organizations vying for representative authority among the Muslim communities of Europe. In that sense, the attempt to mobilize European Muslims had no automatic and simultaneous connection to the demonstrations in the United Kingdom and Islamabad, as Blom would have us believe. The anti-Rushdie protest was certainly an opportunity to give concrete existence to an abstract/imagined sense of community, not unlike the events examined earlier during the Balkan crisis, but it was also coloured by the peculiar situation of the main actors: South Asian Muslims.

Conclusion

Esposito (1997) asserts that 'across the Middle East in the late 1990s, Islam takes many shapes and forms: Islamic republics; illegal opposition organisations and groups; and Islamic movements, from Egypt to Pakistan, engaging in social and political activism and participating within state and society'. The same type of diversity should be applied to European contexts where Islam has been developing, in both public and private ways. The presence on European territory of branches of Islamic movements which moved from the Middle East – or from other countries of origin such as Pakistan or Indonesia – is a European reality about which both academic research as well as public management remain ambiguous.

The followers of Bin Laden are people on the margins, trained and socialized in Islamic networks while being resident in western countries. Those who have been identified and presented by politicians and the media as responsible for the attacks against the US are *de facto* transnational actors: speaking from within any national context, living in the 'periphery' of the Islamic world and committed to multiple conflicts, they do not live in the Middle East (Roy, 2001). Islam is presented by them as a religion (their discourse mobilizes a religious grammar to frame and justify their public action), a dogma, a code, no longer a culture and not – yet – a polity. Roy explains the convergence between these informal networks (potentially active since the end of the 1980s) and based on the movement of militants around the world) and the ongoing nomadism among young Muslims dispersed (not only the western ones) as carrying what he calls a *'cosmopolitan identity'* (2001: 91). Applying this to the European reality, he distinguishes between a 'network of professional activists' manipulated by various types of agencies (secret services, foreign policy-makers, states of origin) and what he refers to as a fundamentalist movement which aims at negotiating with European states for the recognition of maximum rights for the Muslim population. The logic of this binary evolution could be designated the opposition between secrecy and visibility (Roy, 2001: 102–3).

These various figures of Islam do not, however, coexist in the same areas, some are in hospitals or prisons,[40] others are in mosques, schools, women's associations or sport associations. Acting as networks, they capitalize on a number of resources, on the basis of which they develop a capacity for *either* conflict or cooperation between the home country and the territory of residence. This solidarity goes beyond the borders in so far as the identification community to which the *Umma* can correspond to is in fact independent of ties of blood or of soil. The strength of the instrumentalization of a religious (and cultural) repertoire of codes, references, symbols and places in the political domain compensates for the absence of a powerful centralized administration. The model is therefore complex, whereby the transnational dynamics and diasporas, and the interests of the various types of movements examined earlier, do not lead towards to the same type of collective mobilization (Sheffer, 1996; Cohen, 1997; Van Hear, 1998). The structures of decision-making within the organization, the stability of their hierarchies and degree of participation in the countries of origin are variables affecting motivation (Melucci, 1995). Groups mobilize and organize themselves in multiple ways: defensively (in reaction to a threat), offensively (in response to opportunities to carry out the interests of the group in a specific context) or pre-emptively (by anticipating certain occasions and/or forthcoming threats).

One common feature lies in the need to reverse the context of migration from a constraint to a resource. Transnational movement is then represented by the adoption of autonomous networks making it possible to go beyond national political claims and escape the territorial limits in which they are traditionally expressed. The political community remains, but renounces the abstraction of politics, manifesting itself in ways other than those of the liberal vision, allowing activity management and the activation of loyalties and clienteles beyond the borders. The distinction between diasporas and transnational movements is moreover fundamental in so far as it contradicts the hypothesis of a so-called Islamic fifth column, sweeping across the Muslims living in Europe.

The idea of a political community of belonging is still relevant, despite the deterritorialization.[41] It is not even merely an abstraction, rather, it is concretely activated through the various associations we have mentioned in this chapter. Indeed, the networks of associations are quite inventive in finding ways to maintain and strengthen the loyalties beyond borders. This does not, however, mean that transnational movements can be used as an argument demonstrating the existence of a unified and homogeneous Muslim network in Europe. Islam in Europe is a complex series of entities, not a community. September 11, 2001 should prevent any temptation to confuse believers and activists.

Notes

1. Defining political Islam remains a difficult task even after so many scholars have attempted to do so. In this chapter it refers to a convergence of two processes: one aiming to problematize the concept of an integrated society as organized around a religiously based definition of common belonging; the other concerns the willingness to institutionalize this in public life. This definition aims to distinguish between its public manifestation and the private commitment of individuals involved in it.
2. Contexts are characterized by legal methods that enable organization and association. Strategies of action are framed by legal frameworks and provide the opportunity for Muslims to organize themselves in a political space, which would not otherwise sanction them as Muslims. As expressed by Tilly (1978: 55), opportunities cover the relationship between a population and its environment, including power, repression and the articulation between moments of opportunity and threat.
3. The nature of the link which is maintained in the post-migratory era is, however, delicate to qualify. The metaphorical use of the term diaspora considered as transnational minority communities tends to include various categories of population. Dispersed throughout the European territory, the application of this term to the Muslim people of various origins refers less in this case to the traditional idea of a relationship between a centre (territory of origin) and a periphery (places of exile), inherited from the Armenian and Jewish cases, and more to practices coming from the reality of the dispersal; and to transnational operating

modes, indisputably connected to references to a common religious identity (the *Umma*), which is recognized independently of national and ethnic criteria. The religious identification does not constitute the grounding element of a Muslim diaspora, but becomes the structural axis around which the believing community organizes its mobilization or even representation, finding in Europe new opportunities to organize itself.

4. The shock is even bigger for the Europeans as one of the main attackers (of the World Trade Center Twin Towers) resembles the average Muslim living in Europe: speaking the language of the country fluently, educated in one of the best universities and considered a promising student – thus fulfilling the minimum requirements of so-called integration. Did Europe create Mohammed Attah? This has become a frightening question for observers and students of immigration.

5. *Time* ended the year with an issue dedicated to Islam in Europe ('Young Muslims are finding ways to reconcile their traditional faith with Western traditions'), as did other newspapers, such as the *New York Times*, the *International Herald Tribune*, *Corriere della Sera*, *NRC Handelsblad* and *Süddeutsche Zeitung*. In its issue of January 2002, *Courrier International* gathered these articles under a much more ambiguous title: 'Happy as Muslims in Europe?' The various articles presented in the issue reflect the difficulty of assuming a clear position in the face of such a diversified and complex population as the Muslims living in Europe ('Heureux comme les musulmans en Europe?', *Courrier International*, Vol. 586, Nos. 24–30, January 2002, pp. 32–9).

6. On the growing confusion between external and domestic security issues and the construction of 'security continuum' in Europe, see Bigo (1996) and Den Boer (1996).

7. All scholars working on the issue start their analysis with the same statement: it is extremely difficult to establish precisely how many Muslims are living in Europe (meaning in the EU) and to identify the various levels of religious observance. Data are often linked to immigration figures and neglect the growing numbers of Muslims taking the nationality of the country they live in and coming from different countries (Algeria, Morocco, Pakistan, Turkey, Indonesia, etc.). In France, Muslims would number around 4 million, in Germany around 3 million, in the United Kingdom about 2 million, in Italy 800,000, in Spain 600,000, in the Netherlands 400,000 and in Belgium 208,500 (Dassetto et al., 2001). For the first time in April 2001, the Census in Great Britain included a question on religion.

8. Especially if we look at the different experiences European countries had with Islam, and at the various legal arrangements between Islamic organizations/groups and the states, such as a project of an *Intesa* (agreement between the state and a specific community) in Italy, official recognition of Islam in Austria and Belgium) even if 'a European juridical identity exists and this is expressed, to use the words of the Treaty of Maastricht, in a "common constitutional tradition" which constitutes a "general principle of community law"' (Ferrari and Bradney, 2000: 5).

9. Since 1993, Bosnian refugees have been the principal group of asylum applicants, and are largely installed in Northern Westphalia Rhineland. During the first six months of 1998, 11,333 refugees from the former Yugoslavia entered Germany, 72 per cent more than during the first half of 1997 (*Frankfurter Allgemeine Zeitung*, 8 July 1998). A third (35.7 per cent) of the total number of refugees present in Germany originate from former Yugoslavia. A quarter of the 2.5 million Albanians of Kosovo now live abroad (400,000 in Germany), most of them having arrived since 1989–90 (Kumin, 1997).

10. The same principle was later applied to other *Länder* (administrative designation for the regions) such as Bade Würtemberg, Niedersachsen and Bayern.

11. Twenty-five thousand Albanian Kosovars live there, of whom 100 are particularly active in politico-religious activities. It is then possible to identify the principal cities in which their political militantism is deployed: Tübingen, Ludwigsburg, Heilbron and Mosbach.

12. In terms of entrepreneurship, three categories can be distinguished: the (classical) ethnic business in which we include *halal* business, small and medium-sized enterprises (banking, insurance, travel agencies and textiles) and what some authors call the exotic sector, by which they mean enterprises addressed to a larger audience and not exclusively to the strict community.

13. See the bibliography presented in Dassetto et al. (2001).

14. The second edition of Sfeir's (2001) work on Islamist networks in Europe is an excellent illustration of the confusion easily made between this extremely diverse population.

15. In his excellent work on the United Kingdom, Peter Mandaville (2001) refers in particular to the Hizb ul tahriri, which had little political success in the Middle East and great success in the United Kingdom. Coming to Europe, these types of movements enter places where they do not have a history and are then not perceived negatively.

16. '*Dar al-Harb*' is the abode of war; '*Dar al-Islam*' is the abode of Islam; '*Dar al-Shahada*' is the abode of sacrifice in the name of Allah, or martyrdom.

17. Religious groups can be also organized as cultural associations according to the law of 1905. This law limits the possibility of receiving state subsidies.

18. All religious groups are considered equal vis-à-vis each other as well as in their relationship with the state. This right has been extended to other groups, such as the Jewish community.

19. In article 36 of the WRV *Religionsgesellschaften* (society) were mentioned before becoming, in the Fundamental Law in 1949, the *Religionsgemeinschaften* (community). It is furthermore important to make a clear distinction between the *Religionsgemeinschaften* and the *religiöse Vereine* (such as Islamic associations).

20. Acting in networks is the principal resource of this delocalized Islam, helping it in gaining autonomy in relation to the territory of origin. The states themselves participate, while being aware of the limits of their intervention sphere in specific sectors abroad. The impact on the countries of origin, however, remains difficult to evaluate: what, for

instance, is the potential effect of these religious movements, formulated politically and/or culturally dismantled and rebuilt in Europe, on similar segments of populations (in terms of militancy) who remained in the countries of origin?

21. Religious societies are public law agencies, which are allowed to raise taxes.

22. IGMG stands for the Islamische Gesellschaft Milli Gorus, and AK is the Turkish word for welfare (referring to the Welfare Party).

23. This 1994 initiative can be compared to the earlier interest expressed by the Turkish state through the *Diyanet* at the beginning of the 1980s in Germany, in taking control over what the Turkish regime considers deviance from Islamic orthodoxy (at least in its Kemalist conception). This will be elaborated upon later.

24. Interestingly enough, competition with non-Islamic newspapers is ruling the market: *Milli Gazete* (a daily newspaper linked with the Islamist AK [*Adalet ve Kakilnma Partisi*, Justice and Development Party, formerly *AK*] *Partisi* in Turkey) has, for example, been progressively suppressed since 1995 from distribution in European countries, not so much as a consequence of the new (temporary) ruling position in Turkey of the *AK* (Welfare) Party, and a strategy of protection, but due to its failure to compete with more popular daily newspapers.

25. Here I adopt the definition given by Tilly of repertoire as a 'limited set of routines that are learned, shared, and acted through a relatively deliberate process of choices' (Tilly, 1995: 26).

26. The vehement debates on veiling (worn by female lycée school students) of the 1980s and 1990s have helped certain associations to gain visibility and promote themselves as partners for public authorities (Kepel, 2000).

27. For a regular update on the development of these consultations, see the publication of *Istichara* on http://www.interieur.gouv.fr.

28. The German Constitutional Court decided on 15 January 2002 to permit the ritual slaughter of animals by Muslims.

29. The case of Evry's mosque is perhaps the most famous illustration of direct sponsorship by Saudi Arabia through an ad hoc association called Jam'iyyat al Barr wal Takwa li Markaz Evry.

30. *Die Zeit*, 22 August 1996.

31. For more information on France, see Fregosi (1998).

32. The first immigrant from Yugoslavia arrived in 1954 but a proper agreement was signed between Yugoslavia and Germany only in 1968.

33. The AMGT has been in Germany for more than 30 years. It appeared for the first time in 1972, and since then has changed its name several times: Türkische Union Deutschland e.V. in Braunschweig in 1972, then, in November 1976 in Cologne, the Türkische Union Europa, on 22 October 1983 the Islamische Union Europa e.V. before taking, on 20 May 1985, Avrupa Milli Görüs Teskilatlari's name (AMGT-Vereinigung der Neuen Weltsicht in Europa e.V. – Association of the new national vision in Europe). AMGT activities were advanced in Germany during the short period in which the Milli Salamet (MSP) took part in the coalition (three times between 1974 and 1979). During the last stage of the history of the patronym, at the conference of 3 June 1995 in Frankfurt, the AMGT

was divided into two sub-organizations: the Islamische Gesellschaft Milli Görüs (IGMG) dedicated to political and social work, and the Europäische Moscheebau– und Unterstützungs Gemeinschaft e.V. (EMUG) devoted to finance and to property (in particular mosques); while developing two types of speech, one political, the other cultural, for the attention of two separate populations.

34. The Geopolitical Observatory for Drugs considers Albanians the most active in drug dealing (Lipsius, 1998).

35. The BVS-Berlin's president publicly denounced in 1997 the potential violence among Islamic groups settled in Germany, referring explicitly to Hamas and Hizbollah, and noting the incompatibility between Islam and German Fundamental Law, as reported in *Tagesspiegel*, 29 September 1997.

36. Statistisches Landesamt Baden-Württemberg, 31 December 1996.

37. On 1 November 1997, the reopening of the schools and universities in Kosovo was celebrated in Stuttgart with demonstrations expressing solidarity with the students' protest movements which helped this process.

38. The Turkish case is a good illustration of this mechanism. The beginning of 1994 witnessed a scandal concerning the diversion of money collected in Germany and Europe for the Muslims of Bosnia, to profit the election campaign of the AK (Amiraux, 2001). The Internationale Humanistische Hilfe e.V. was the central association for collecting funds. It is based in a mosque of the AMGT in Freiburg. There was no legal link between these organizations, but it was often the same people working on both sides: the president of the association managing the mosque was also the vice-president of the humanitarian body. On the whole, around DM 1.4 million was raised and transferred from Germany to Turkey, while an equivalent amount was collected in Turkey.

39. 'Every single Kosovo citizen has a moral duty to give up 3% of his/her salary to the Foundation for Kosovo,' points out *Le Monde*, 2–3 August 1998. The estimation regarding the amount of money raised is pure speculation.

40. Speaking of prisons in England and Wales, Beckford and Gilliat point out the inequalities of treatment between Christian prisoners and prisoners from other confessions: 'The reason why the issue of equal opportunities for religion has become so important in prison is that it arises out of a major point of tension between the State, the Church of England and other faiths. It is an issue which epitomizes and, by virtue of being an extreme case of a general phenomenon, clarifies some of the underlying difficulties facing the UK's transition to a religious mixed society' (1998: 3).

41. It is interesting to note that the 'territorialization' of ethnicity and its use in public discourse in France is part of an attempt to grapple with the complex reality of European Islam. Young Muslims living in peripheral urban settings, for example, are labelled '*jeunes des quartiers*', especially in the press. This way of referencing is increasingly adopted by politicians, as was evident during the 2002 presidential campaigns.

References

Allievi, Stefano. *Les convertis à l'Islam. Les nouveaux musulmans d'Europe* (Paris: L'Harmattan, 1998).
—— and Dassetto, Felice. *Il ritorno dell'Islam: I musulmani in Italia* (Rome: Lavoro, 1993).
Amiraux, Valérie. 'Les limites du transnational comme espace de mobilisation', *Cultures & Conflicts*, September 1999, pp. 25–50.
—— *Acteurs de l'islam entre Allemagne et Turquie. Parcours militants et expériences religieuses*, (Paris: L'Harmattan [Collection Logiques Politiques], 2001).
Basdevant-Gaudemet, Brigitte. 'The Legal Status of Islam in France', in Silvio Ferrari and Anthony Bradney (eds.). *Islam and European Legal Systems* (Dartmouth: Ashgate, 2000), pp. 97–124.
Beckford, James and Gilliat, Sophie. *Religion in Prison: Equal Rites in a Multi-Faith Society* (Cambridge: Cambridge University Press, 1998).
Bellion Jourdan, Jerôme. 'Les organisations de secours islamique et l'action humanitaire', *Esprit*, No. 277, August–September 2001, pp. 173–85.
Bigo, Didier. *Polices en réseaux: l'expérience européenne* (Paris: Presses de la Fondation Nationale des Sciences, Politiques, 1996).
—— 'The Möbius Ribbon of Internal and External Security', in Albert Mathias, Jacobson David and Yosef Lapid (eds.). *Identities, Borders, Orders: Rethinking International Relations Theory* (Minneapolis: University of Minnesota Press, 2001), pp. 91–116.
Binswanger, Karl and Sipahioglu, Fethi. *Türkisch-islamische Vereine als Faktor deutsch-türkischer Koexistenz* (Munich: Benediktbeuren, 1988).
Blom, Amélie. 'Is There Such a Thing as "Global Belonging"? Transnational Protest during the "Rushdie Affair"', in Andrew Geddes and Adrian Favell (eds.). *The Politics of Belonging: Migrants and Minorities in Contemporary Europe* (Aldershot: Ashgate, 1999), pp. 192–208.
Bougarel, Xavier and Clayer, Nathalie. *Le nouvel islam balkanique: les musulmans, acteurs du post-communisme, 1990–2000* (Paris: Maisonneuve et Larose, 2001).
Burgat, François. *L'Islamisme en face* (Paris: La Découverte, 1995, reprinted in 2002).
Calic, Marie Janine. 'Kosovo: Krieg oder Konfliktlösung?' *Südosteuropa Mitteilungen*, February 1998, pp. 112–23.
Cesari, Jocelyne. *Musulmans et républicains: Les jeunes, l'islam et la France* (Brussels: Complexe, 1998).
—— 'Diasporas as Transnational Networks in the Context of Globalization', Conference Paper MIG/40 Florence, 8–9 May 1998.
Cohen, Robin. *Global Diasporas. An Introduction* (London: UCL Press, 1997).
Dassetto, Felice. *La construction de l'Islam européen: approche socio-anthropologique* (Paris: L'Harmattan, 1996).
—— and Bastenier, Albert. *L'Islam transplanté* (Anvers: EPO, 1984).
—— and Bastenier, Albert. *Immigration et espace public: la controverse de l'intégration* (Paris: L'Harmattan, 1993).
—— Maréchal, Brigitte and Nielsen, Jorgen. *Convergences musulmanes: Aspects contemporains de l'Islam dans l'Europe élargie* (Louvain-la-Neuve: Bruylant-Academia et L'Harmattan, 2001).

Den Boer, Monica. 'Justice and Home Affairs: Cooperation without Integration', in Wallace, Helen and Wallace, William (eds.). *Policy-Making in the European Union* (Oxford: Oxford University Press, 1996), pp. 389–409.

Esposito. John. *Political Islam: Revolution, Radicalism or Reform?* (Boulder, Colorado: Lynne Rienner, 1997).

Etzioni, Amitai. *The Active Society: A Theory of Societal and Political Processes* (London: Collier-Macmillan, 1968).

Ferrari, Silvio and Bradney, Anthony (eds.). *Islam and European Legal Systems* (Dartmouth: Ashgate, 2000).

Fregosi, Franck. *La formation des cadres religieux musulmans en France: approches socio-juridiques* (Paris: L'Harmattan, 1998).

Gerholm, Tomas, and Lithman, Yngve G. (eds.). *The New Islamic Presence in Western Europe* (London: Mansell, 1988).

Ghalioun, Burhan. *Islam et politique* (Paris: La Découverte, 1997).

Guiraudon, Virginie. *Les politiques d'immigration en Europe: Allemagne, France, Pays-Bas* (Paris: L'Harmattan [Collection Logiques Politiques], 2000).

Haddad, Yvonne Yazbeck. 'Towards the Carving of Islamic Space in "the West"', *ISIM Newsletter*, 1998.

Hartmann, Thomas and Krannich, Margret (eds.). *Muslime in sakulären rechstaat. Neue Akteure in Kultur und Politik* (Berlin: das Arabische Buch, 2001).

Heitmeyer, Wilhelm, Müller, Joachim and Schröder, Helmut (eds.). *Verlockender Fundamentalismus: türkische Jugendliche in Deutschland* (Frankfurt am Main: Suhrkamp, 1997).

Helga, Walter. 'Verfassungsrechtliche Probleme der muslimischen Glaubens-gemeinschaften in der BRD', in Einar von Schuler (Hrsg.), *XIII. deutscher Orientalistentag vom 16. bis 20. September 1985. Ausgewählte Vorträge* (Stuttgart: Franz Steiner Verlag Wiebaden Gmbh, 1989), pp. 192–9.

Höfert, Almut and Armando, Salvatore (eds.). *Between Europe and Islam. Shaping Modernity in a Transcultural Space* (Brussels: Peter Lang, 2000).

Jonker, Gerdien and Sakaranaho, Tuula (eds). 'Female Inroads into Muslim Communities: Reconstructions of Knowledge, Community, and Communication', 2003, *Social Compass* 2003/1.

Jordi, Moreras. *Musulmanes en Barcelona: Espacios y dinámicas comunitarias* (Barcelona: CIDOB Edicions, 1999).

Katzenstein, Peter J. *Policy and Politics in West Germany. The Growth of a Semisovereign State* (Philadelphia, Pennsylvania: Temple University Press, 1987).

Kepel, Gilles. *Les banlieues de l'Islam: naissance d'une religion en France* (Paris: Seuil, 1987).

—— *Jihad: Expansion et déclin de l'islamisme* (Paris: Gallimard, 2000).

—— and Leveau, Rémy. *Les musulmans dans la société française* (Paris: Presses de la FNSP, 1988).

Khosrokhavar, Farhad. *L'Islam des jeunes* (Paris: Flammarion, 1997).

Koopmans, Ruud. 'Globalization or Still National Politics? A Comparison of Protests against the Gulf War in Germany, France, and the Netherlands', in Donatella Della Porta, Hanspeter Kriesi and Rucht Dieter (eds.). *Social Movements in a Globalizing World* (London: Macmillan, 1999), pp. 57–70.

Krasner, Stephen D. 'Power Politics, Institutions, and Transnational Relations', in Thomas Risse-Kappen, *Bringing Transnational Relations Back In: Non-State Actors, Domestic Structures and International Institutions* (Cambridge: Cambridge University Press, 1995), pp. 257–79.

Kumin, Judith. 'Rückkehr der Flüchtlinge nach Bosnien-Herzegowina', *Südosteuropa Mitteilungen*, No. 2, 1997, pp. 75–8.

Landman, Nico. *Van mat tot minaret: de institutionalisering van de islam in Nederland* (Amsterdam: VU-Uitgeverij, 1992).

Lewis, Philip. *Islamic Britain: Religion, Politics and Identity among British Muslims: Bradford in the 1990s* (London: I.B. Tauris, 1994; 2nd edition, 2002).

Lipsius, Stephan. 'Untergrundsorganisationen in Kosovo', *Südosteuropa Mitteilungen*, vol. CXVII, Nos. 1–2, January 1998, pp. 75–82.

MacAdam, Doug and Snow, David. *Social Movements* (Los Angeles: Roxbury Publishing Company, 1997).

Mandaville, Peter. *Transnational Muslim Politics: Reimagining the Umma* (London: Routledge, 2001).

Maunz, Theodor, Durig, Günter and Herzog, Roman. *Kommentar Zum Grundgesetz* (Munich: C.H. Beck Verlag, 1994).

Melucci, Alberto. 'The Process of Collective Identity', in Hank Johnston and Bert Klandermans (eds.). *Social Movements and Culture* (Minneapolis, University of Minnesota Press, 1995), pp. 41–63.

Münz, Rainer, Wolfgang, Seifert and Ralf, Ulrich (eds.). *Zuwanderung nach Deutschland. Strukturen, Wirkungen, Perspektiven* (Frankfurt am Main: Campus Verlag, 1997).

Nielsen, Jorgen, 'British Responses to 11 September', *ISIM Newsletter*, September 2002, p. 16.

Nonneman, Gerd, Niblock, Tim and Szajkowski, Bogdan (eds.). *Muslim Communities in the New Europe* (Reading: Ithaca Press, 1996).

Rath, J., Sunier, T. and Meyer, A. 'Islam in the Netherlands. The Establishment of Islamic Institutions in a De-pillarizing Society', *Tijdschrift voor Economische en Sociale Geografie/Journal of Economic and Social Geography*, 1997, 88 (4), pp. 389–95.

Risse-Kappen, Thomas. *Bringing Transnational Relations Back In: Non-State Actors, Domestic Structures and International Institutions* (Cambridge: Cambridge University Press, 1995).

Robbers, Gerhard. 'The Legal Status of Islam in Germany', in Silvio Ferrari and Anthony Bradney (eds.). *Islam and European Legal Systems* (Dartmouth: Ashgate, 2000), pp. 147–53.

Rokkan, Stein. *Citizens, Elections, Parties* (Oslo: Universitetsforlaget, 1970).

Roy, Olivier. 'Le neo-fondamentalisme islamique ou l'imaginaire de l'Oummah', *Esprit*, April 1996, pp. 80–107.

—— *Vers un Islam Européen* (Paris: Esprit, 1999).

—— 'Muslims in Europe: From Ethnic Identity to Religious Recasting', *ISIM Newsletter*, 2000, p. 5.

—— *Généalogie de l'islamisme* (Paris: Hachette, 2001, 2nd edition).

Schiffauer, Werner. *Die Bauern von Subay – Das Leben in einem türkischen Dorf* (Stuttgart: Klett-Cotta, 1987).

—— *Die Migranten aus Subay – Türken in Deutschland: Eine Ethnographie* (Stuttgart: Klett-Cotta, 1991).

—— *Die Gottesmänner: Türkische Islamisten in Deutschland* (Frankfurt am Main: Suhrkamp, 2000).

Sfeir, Antoine. *Les réseaux d'Allah: les filieres islamistes en France et en Europe* (Paris: Plon, 1997, 2nd edition, 2001).

Shadid, Wasif and van Koningsveld, Peter (eds.). *The Integration of Islam and Hinduism in Western Europe* (Kampen: Kok Pharos, 1991).

—— (eds). *Muslims in the Margin: Political Responses to the Presence of Islam in Western Europe* (Kampen: Kok Pharos, 1996).

Sheffer, Gabi. 'Wither the Study of Ethnic Diasporas? Some Theoretical, Definitional, Analytical and Comparative Considerations', in Georges Prévélakis (ed.). *The Networks of Diasporas* (Paris: L'Harmattan, 1996), pp. 37–46.

Soysal, Yasemin. *Limits of Citizenship* (Chicago: Chicago University Press, 1994).

Tibi, Bassam. *The Challenge of Fundamentalism: Political Islam and New World Disorder* (Berkeley: University of California Press, 1998).

Tilly, Charles. *From Mobilization to Revolution* (Reading, Mass.: Addison-Wesley, 1978).

Thränhardt, Dietrich. `Regionale Ansätze und Schwerpunktaufgaben der Integration von Migrantinnen und Migranten in Nordrhein-Westfalen', Studie im Auftrag des Ministeriums für Umwelt, Raumordung und Lanwirtschaft des Landes Nordrhein-Westfalen, 1998.

Van Hear, Nicholas. *New Diasporas: The Mass Exodus, Dispersal and Regrouping of Migrant Communities* (London: UCL Press, 1998).

Vertovec, Steven and Peach, Ceri (eds.). *Islam in Europe: The Politics of Religion and Community* (Basingstoke: Macmillan, 1997).

Walter, Helga. Verfassungsrechtliche Probleme der muslimischen Glaubensgemeinschaften in der BRD', in Einar von Schuler (ed.). *XIII. deutscher Orientalistentag*, Vol. 16, No. 20, September 1989: Ausgewälte Vortrage (Stuttgart: Franz Steiner Verlag Gmbh, 1989), pp. 192–9.

3
Political Islam in Sweden: Integration and Deterrence

Jan Hjärpe

Introduction

If we define 'political Islam' as certain ideologies using Islam to play a decisive role in the political system of a state, then the phenomenon is hardly conceivable in Sweden. But if we pose the question of the relevance of transnational political Islam to the Muslim presence in Northern Europe, it becomes more interesting. Such a presence, in turn, is related to general economic, social and political events. Another interesting feature concerns the relationship between Swedish foreign and domestic policy and political Islam in the Muslim world – and particularly to 'jihadist' Islamism, i.e. militant groups accepting violence and terror as religiously legitimate methods – on the one hand, and Swedish policy vis-à-vis Islamism after September 11, 2001 on the other.

In the mid-1990s, the Swedish government initiated a Euro-Islam project administered by the Foreign Ministry and the Swedish Institute (a non-governmental body concerned with cultivating international cultural contacts), focusing on the relations between European and Islamic cultures, and the position of Muslims in Europe. The first meeting under the auspices of this project took place in 1995 in Stockholm (15–17 June).[1] One of the aims was to include Islamists, based on the acceptance that Islamism (or political Islam) constituted a reality that needed to be acknowledged in order to contribute to the strengthening of democratic dialogue and to the development of competing groups and interests in the Muslim world. The reaction among secular Muslims in Sweden was negative: they maintained that only those engaged in Islamic organizations in Sweden (and were not of Islamist orientation) functioned as representatives of the Muslim presence in the country. There was also an adverse response from those who preferred to follow a policy of exclusion towards Islamists and Iran, which would also be represented in the conference. Should 'extremists' be invited and engaged in the debate, or should they be excluded and banned from international contacts of this kind? It is quite clear that opinions on this were very polarized in the Swedish political debate, and the 1990s witnessed an oscillation between the two policies, inclusivism versus exclusivism.

There was a second conference on Euro-Islam, organized in cooperation with Jordan, in Mafraq, 10–13 June 1996.[2] Sweden had promised an engagement focusing on culture and cultural manifestations within the so-called Barcelona Process of the European Union, and aiming at enhancing cooperation among the countries in the Mediterranean region. A workshop (mainly for diplomats) was arranged in Stockholm on 23 and 24 April 1998, entitled the 'Dialogue between Cultures and Civilizations'.[3] These two ventures were adversely impacted, due to 'oscillation' between including or excluding the moderate Islamist voices. In any event, it is clear that the government of Prime Minister Göran Persson has adopted a more 'exclusivist' policy than that of his predecessor Ingvar Carlsson, and did not express an equivalent interest in Euro-Mediterranean cultural cooperation.

After the events of September 11, 2001, the prime minister of the Social Democratic government and political parties to the right have supported the US Administration's stance with regard to the 'war against terrorism' and the bombing of Afghanistan. This position came under considerable criticism from sections of the Social Democrat Party, as well as the political left, NGOs and Sweden's intellectual elite. The criticism focused on the abuse of human rights, legal procedures and international conventions. But another consequence of the war against terrorism rhetoric has been an increasing awareness of the distinction between 'jihadist', or violent, Islamism and more moderate political Islam. Not only that, but there is also a realization of the difference between Islamism as a political movement on the one hand, and mainstream Muslim piety on the other.

Historic Relations and Developments

In the 1990s conferences, as well as at other occasions of contact and dialogue, a rhetoric developed in which earlier relations between Scandinavia and the Muslim world featured. These have a long history. Among the most frequently evoked symbols of these exchanges are the large numbers of coins from the era of the Vikings, found in what are today the Nordic countries. Most of these are Arab coins from Abbasid times. The coins have become a symbol, used in the discourse of Nordic Arabists as well as by politicians, during various cultural exchange celebrations. In the 1980s a special exhibition of such coins went on tour in the major cities of the Arab countries, accompanied by other cultural activities, in order to promote Swedish diplomatic and commercial initiatives.

Another symbol of these early relations are runic inscriptions on Viking tombstones and menhirs (memorial stones) which explicitly mention Särkland, the land of the Saracens. A third symbol, also often quoted, are stories about Nordic merchants by Arab authors of the time, especially Ibn Fadlan.[4]

In reality the Viking era was a short interlude, and in this context its value is rhetorical. Nevertheless, for Muslim immigrants and their children, the archaeological evidence of such early links has a cognitive function in their integration in Swedish society: these contacts are old – older than the Swedish state as a political and administrational entity – and they were of a peaceful and commercial nature.

During the Middle Ages the European North came under the dominance of the Catholic Church. When the Scandinavian countries began to emerge, they were on the periphery of the Mediterranean culture. Direct contacts with the Muslim world became rare. The Reformation in the sixteenth century can be regarded as the emancipation of the North from the dominance of southern Europe. The Scandinavian countries (as well as the other countries of the Reformation) became political, economic and cultural entities in their own right. But this also meant a degree of isolation, and contacts with the Muslim world thus became sporadic.

The participation of Scandinavians in the Crusades was minimal. This too is of importance today, particularly with regard to the current discourse and worldview of contemporary Islamist movements. The latter regard the European colonialism of the nineteenth and twentieth centuries and current US hegemony as a 'crusade', and see the Crusades of the Middle Ages to today's events and dynamics as a continuum.[5] This was even echoed in the videos made by Osama Bin Laden after September 11, 2001, and has been a constant theme in his various addresses.

In Swedish history there was another factor behind the establishment of new contacts with the Muslim world in the eighteenth century: the threat from an expanding Russia, striving to reach the

Baltic and the Black Sea. During the entire eighteenth century a military alliance was in force between the Ottoman Empire with its Caliphate (seat of power) in Istanbul and the Swedish state governed from Stockholm. The Swedish National Archives contain a multitude of Ottoman Turkish documents dating from this period of military and diplomatic initiatives against Russia. Another surviving feature of that time is the Swedish Consulate General in Istanbul, which now houses the Swedish Research Institute. This too has a rhetorical value in the discourse on Islam and Sweden, as does the recently established Swedish Institute in Alexandria.

The eighteenth century was also a period of commercial treaties concluded with the states of northern Africa, in addition to scientific and scholarly expeditions to various parts of the Muslim world. Although tourism in the nineteenth century was confined largely to the upper classes, we nevertheless find migration for work taking place during this period. The latter phenomenon was visible in the form of skilled workers from Scandinavia emigrating to the Ottoman regions of eastern Europe and North Africa. This is also the period of the first Swedish Quranic translations and of learned Orientalist works.[6] These facts play a role in contradicting the dualist worldview characteristic of much of the Islamist discourse which has a tendency to essentialize a division between 'Islam' and the 'West'.

The Scandinavian countries in the nineteenth and early twentieth centuries were homogeneous entities. This was to change.[7] The process of secularization meant a relatively different political role for religion as compared with its earlier function, when religious affiliation was a national marker and regarded as the ideological foundation of society, and the established church was a tool in the administration of the state.[8] Religion functioned very much as a legitimation of power. In the twentieth century, however, this was supplanted by the concept of the 'popular mandate', that is, democracy. Secularization coincided with industrialization and technological development, and later with the creation of the welfare state, when citizenship became a valuable asset. Citizenship enabled the individual to be part of a welfare system regardless of confessional affiliation, and with the religious communities playing a limited social or economic role. Indeed, from the 1960s onwards, the very concept of 'Sweden' was synonymous with a common language, civil rights, egalitarianism and welfare. These constituted what became known as the 'the Swedish model'.

The development of this kind of welfare society coincided with the arrival of a Muslim presence in Sweden. In the early 1930s the number of Muslims in the country, according to an official census, was under 15, which in reality means that there was no discernible Muslim presence at all. The first group, which was still numerically small (less than 100) was composed of Tatars, who came from Finland and Estonia during the Second World War, some as refugees and some as work migrants. These people formed an association in Stockholm in 1949, with activities including Islamic religious education and other religious services. Initially, the objective of the association was to maintain a sense of belonging and ethnic cohesion. At that stage, it is difficult to decipher any traces of a more politicized form of Islam. Later, as a result of the immigration of people of other ethnic descent, who soon outnumbered the Tatars, the association developed more specifically into a religious community (Islam Församlingen i Sverige).[9] This also meant changes in its outlook, although still within the context of a modern secular welfare state.

Contemporary Dynamics and Challenges

The development of a welfare state system, which was made possible due to the economic affluence of the 1950s and the fact that Sweden had not been directly involved in the Second World War, meant an increased demand for labour. Muslim immigrants in the 1960s and early 1970s were thus so-called guestworkers in factories, and therefore not only welcomed, but actively recruited from Yugoslavia (including Bosnia) and Turkey. Their integration was relatively trouble-free, and the question of any separate religious status was quite simply not on the agenda.

A change came in tandem with increased immigration in the 1980s and 1990s, consisting almost entirely of refugees seeking safety and asylum from discrimination, war and other disasters. This in itself constituted a problem: this immigration was not in response to a need for labour power, and there was already a comparatively high rate of unemployment. They were thus regarded as an economic problem by some in politics, and opinions pressing for change in immigration policies were voiced. The social marginalization of these immigrants became almost inevitable, and this was (and still is) quite often expressed as due to differences in 'culture' or 'religion'.

These developments were portrayed clearly in the media during the 1980s and 1990s, for instance in the 'letters to the editor' sections of the newspapers and in opinion polls.[10] Also contributing to the bad press on Islam during this period were the ongoing conflicts in the Muslim world: the civil war in Lebanon, the Iraq–Kuwait conflict, Kashmir separatism, and so on, and the connection between certain Islamist movements and violent actions (whereby religious arguments were used by some of these movements to legitimize their violence).

For the general public, it was – and still is – not easy to distinguish between the rhetoric of such violent movements, and the (different kinds of) Islam practised by the immigrants in Sweden. Among the latter, therefore, was a need to mark this distinction explicitly, that is, to disavow political Islam. This was clearly the policy of the established Muslim groups and of religious leaders after the World Trade Center disaster.

There has been a considerable change in the Muslim presence in Sweden over the last 20 years. However, since religious affiliation is not registered and there is no official census, all the figures are more or less qualified guesswork. There are, in fact, huge discrepancies, since the numbers are dependent on how religious affiliation (such as activity, membership in organizations, actual practice, ethnicity or names) is defined. We can find numbers quoted varying from 60,000 to 300,000, the first being too low and the latter too high.[11] Nevertheless, it is undeniable that there is a considerable presence. It is interesting to note that even this statistical insecurity has to do with the welfare state, where registration of religious affiliation is regarded as an infringement of an individual's privacy and counterproductive to social integration. As a consequence, religious affiliation often comes low on a hierarchy of norms or identities, compared with professional identity, family membership, engagement in sport activities, and so on.

The welfare state system has consequences for the role of religions in general, and in turn influences the actual functioning of religious communities – and thereby also the concept of what 'religion' is – and what constitutes a religious community. In a functioning welfare state the individual derives her/his basic security (for example, security of life and property and health care) by virtue of their citizenship, and can access social and political rights regardless of ethnicity, class or religious affiliation (if any). In effect, s/he works within the framework of the legislation of the state, where the state is strong enough to implement this (secular) legislation. This means very concretely that s/he marries (or does not marry) the spouse of her/his choice (since the state guarantees the security and support of the children, stability in the relationship is not necessary). In addition, s/he gets a state pension, which means not being dependent on children (if any) in old age, or on relatives or religious communities.

This in effect means a significant change in the roles traditionally allotted to family and/or clan, and this particularly impacts on immigrant families. Indeed, generational tensions and/or conflicts among immigrant families sometimes result in violence. Some men in particular have reacted violently when young women have opted for a lifestyle different from the one chosen for them by their families.[12] In some cases, crimes such as 'honour killings' have taken place. Women have chosen spouses whom their family have regarded as undesirable, or in other ways departed from the traditional codes of behaviour, and the father, husband or brother has killed the woman and explicitly argued in mitigation in court that it was necessary to do so in order to restore the honour of the family. Much attention has been given to these cases in the media. Of special political consequence was the murder of Fadime Sahindal, a Kurd, on 21 January 2002. Conflict with her father had received some media coverage, particularly since she was politically active. Her father had already been sentenced for threatening Fadime after she had chosen to leave her family home and live independently, or with a boyfriend, at which point she had made public statements. The father, after pressure from relatives, shot her. The reaction from the political establishment was very emphatic, and representatives from the royal family and the government attended her funeral. The service was also broadcast on national television. It was regarded as a national event and became the impetus for the state to undertake a number of measures to attempt to prevent similar killings in the future. There was a perceptible change in public debates and questions of 'cultural norms', previously regarded as politically incorrect, became more frequent and common.

The state has the power not only to legislate but to enforce its laws. These laws are not eternal, nor do they necessarily possess any divine nature or validity, but they are applied as a result of the strength of the state and its administrative apparatus.[13] One can assume that if the state is able to provide this welfare system and guarantee to support the individual, there is little appeal in the idea of a divine law or a theocratic state order. Indeed, among Muslim intellectuals and professionals in Sweden, a common argument in the discussions on the role of religion and state, which took place in the 1960s and 1970s – and remains ongoing – is that it is conceivable to interpret the welfare system and secular legislation as harmonious with (or even as an expression of) true Islam. In other words, the secular welfare system and contemporary legislation are much more 'Islamic' than either the actual systems found in the Muslim world, and/or the ideology of the 'Mawdudi-type' Islamists. The latter are movements which have been inspired by or related to the ideas of the Pakistani Islamist Abul Ala Mawdudi (d. 1979), resulting in his own organization, the Jamaat-i-Islami, in addition to movements such as al-Ikhwan al-Muslimun (the Muslim Brotherhood) in the Arabic world. A characteristic trait is the view that Islam in itself constitutes a very specific blueprint for the state.

There are other communities in Swedish society besides those represented by the official sector, or those constituted by citizenship and membership in the local municipality. These other communities include religious groups, churches, denominations, sects and cults. Individuals, however, can choose whether to take any of these or ignore them. In other words, they are not essential for the survival of the individual.

Hence, religion is viewed and defined narrowly, and is regarded as belonging to the sphere of individual free choice. One consequence is that a concept of religion regarded as social order, or connected to a special legal status (a ghetto, or *millet* system where the group belonging constitutes an essential feature in the individual's possibilities to have a career and survive), does not fit easily into the present structure of society. Religion can still be regarded as 'a comprehensive system' – but only for the individual and by her/his own choice.

It is difficult to actualize a more collective notion of religion, as evidenced, for instance, by attempts to establish Islamic schools. Most of these attempts have failed, partly because of a lack of interest from the intended 'market'. This limited definition of religion – as unrelated to legal status and interpretation – would be difficult to grasp by Islamists who stress a traditional Islamic understanding of their faith as a system of life (including *fiqh* – jurisprudence) and of governance, that is, *din wa dawla* (loosely translated as religion and state).

Muslim refugees in Sweden do not come from countries which could in any way be described as welfare states. On the contrary, in many instances the state and its institutions have been unable to provide security for them, leading to an exodus of people in search of asylum elsewhere. The scenario runs thus: an individual who has previously been dependent on social relations other than the state for her/his needs, protection and help becomes a refugee and/or migrant who will then go to a country with a welfare state structure. As a rule, s/he does not abandon the religious affiliation (the notable exception being certain Iranian refugees with anti-religious attitudes), but the notions of 'family' and of 'religion' become problematic as their actual functions change in the Swedish environment.

One of the repercussions of this is the frequently observed phenomenon of tension between new immigrants and earlier, well-integrated minority groups, meaning those individuals who have built careers, made inroads into society and participate actively in political and cultural life. Such is the case, for instance, with the well-established Jewish communities in Sweden.

The role of religion as an ethnic marker becomes weaker as the process of integration advances. Muslims in Sweden still differ according to how Islam features in their respective countries of origin. But for non-believers, religious affiliation ceases to be of importance, and would have little, if any, impact on concerns regarding personal legal status in their 'new' country. Overall, religion as an ethnic identifier becomes increasingly less important. Thus, customs and habits, clothes and rituals, which in previous environments had the function of showing that one was 'like everyone else', now have the opposite function: they show that one is 'unlike others', and a distinction is made between what is 'customary' and what is 'religious'. Islam becomes a matter of personal belief and less of tradition, particularly as the functioning structures of a society with a considerably strong administration, decide the conditions and influence the frameworks of Muslim institutions, local communities and organizations on the national level.

The result is that different Muslim groups organize themselves into what might be compared to denominations, or organizational structures according to a distinct Swedish tradition, which does not correspond to organizational structures in Muslim countries. There are, for instance, a number of Muslim umbrella organizations at the national level, with differing tendencies (traditionalist, modernist, with different attitudes to Sufism, a deeply spiritual Muslim tradition, or to political Islam), including a special Bosnian Muslim organization with its own European Islamic tradition.[14] Consequently, it is impossible to apply religion as principally a social order or a juridical/legal system, as this would be unacceptable within the context of the integration policies of the Swedish state; nor does it conform to the government's conditions for support for religious organizations.

As a result, on a practical level, the concept of *fiqh* (jurisprudence derived from Islamic sources and traditions, and used to guide and judge social behaviour) becomes supplanted by the notion of personal 'moral values'. And religion is no longer either a moral or social order, but rather a matter of a individual choice.[15] Most people from a Muslim background choose not to practise their religion very diligently as a means of assimilating into the new society, where 'religion' has a low priority. However, there are aspects of Islam, such as those stressing personal religious experience, which correspond to the expectations of Swedish society in terms of what 'religion' should be. *Tasawwuf* (religion as experience or mysticism), fits better than the idea of a Divine Law applied as a legal system, that is, shari'a, into the concept of religiosity prevailing in Swedish society. While the so-called Tablighi (originating from the Indian Peninsula in the 1920s) and Turkish Süleymaniye movements (both combining social and political in their orientation) have had some impact, one nevertheless finds a considerable number rejecting religion entirely.

Muslim immigrants in Sweden come from very different ethnic, social and educational backgrounds. Hence it becomes necessary to distinguish between Muslim identity and ethnic identity, and between 'Islam' as a system of faith, and the values, habits and customs in the traditional environment (many of which were once regarded as 'Islamic' and taken for granted by the immigrants). What thus occurs is that frames of reference change, resulting in new interpretations or newer ways of viewing one's religion – new, at least, to the individual, who often experiences the process as the discovery of 'true Islam'. Previously popular patterns of Islamic observance come to be regarded as distorted forms of religion.

In observing this process, one would expect that this gives an opportunity for the emergence of Islamism as one of these new interpretations. But the fact is that such a development is very rare, and indeed other manifestations take over. 'Swedish' forms of Islam emerge, leading, on the one hand, to a certain polarization between Muslim groups and individuals, but, on the other to integration in society. In other words, we see the development of various kinds of 'blue-and-yellow Islam'.[16] Effectively, practising Muslims develop into denominations, which coexist with others within the framework of the secular state. Islamists of the type that argue for or espouse 'jihad' are thus few and far between.

So is there no room for political Islam to develop? Jonas Otterbeck has studied the development of a Muslim publication – *Salaam* magazine – in the context of a larger thesis that touches on this question. He analyses in considerable detail changes in the magazine's content, layout, editorial policy and literary style, all in relation to ongoing global processes and different global Islamic trends.[17] The magazine and the organization to which it has been connected (Islamiska informationsföreningen),[18] have clear connections with the Islamic Foundation in Leicester, which in turn has ideological links with the Pakistani Islamist Party (Jamaat-i-Islami), going back to the influence of Abul Ala Mawdudi (see above). This makes it possible to argue that the magazine did have Islamist ideological tendencies or sympathies.

However, one of the most interesting results of Otterbeck's study is his elucidation of the successive changes in the outlook and ideological direction of the magazine, as well as the personal developments among the writers (which resulted in some conflict and changes in the staff). Otterbeck points out the changes that took place: from a '*Mawdudist*' trend to one that stresses religion as a personal engagement, to the inclusion of Sufism within the realm of accepted Islam, and even to an emphasis on the importance of engagement in ecological problems (i.e. Islam as the 'green' religion). Among the younger generation of religiously engaged Muslims in Sweden there is a growing tendency to be engaged in the protection of the environment and to have a sympathy for the 'greens' in political life. This trend has also been the object of special studies.[19]

It is interesting to note that one of those previously engaged in writing for *Salaam*, Pernilla Ouis, a graduate student in Human Ecology, also belongs to a category of academically renowned Muslims taking an increasing part in public debates.[20] This highlights a growing competence on the part of the editorial staff, which points to the fact that the need for material ideological guidance from Leicester has dwindled. This in turn is also a feature of the process of integration into Swedish society. In other words, to be taken seriously as a part of a general public debate also means that the political engagement is centred on concrete questions, be they of special interest for a Muslim community (building mosques or schools, promoting the dissemination of new translations of the Qur'an, and so on) or problems of society as a whole.

There are Muslim members in all the established Swedish political parties. The idea of the Muslim community as a separate body, with its own distinct political ideology (which stands in opposition to the existing Swedish and/or Western ones), is impractical. In addition, Muslims in Sweden do not constitute a homogeneous community, but one that contains different tendencies and interests. This diversity will remain and grow in the future, and should be seen as legitimate variations and expressions of living Islam.

It should also be borne in mind that there is a generational change that belies different frames of mind, between those who came as migrants and the younger Muslims born and educated in the Swedish state school system. It is very interesting to follow the candid debate between young engaged Muslims of different trends on the Internet.[21] One can observe the fact that the feeling of 'belonging' to whatever body or group and actual connections, contacts, relations and cognitive networks today are by no means restricted to the geographical neighbourhood. Sweden has a very high density of personal computers per capita, and the young generation has become highly computer-literate at school. To be in contact with brothers and sisters in faith is thus easy, but so is connecting with each other as youth on common issues regardless of their faith.

A Separate Community?

The whole question of confessional schools, especially Muslim ones, has been analysed by Elisabeth Gerle.[22] As she shows, the debate on separate Islamic schools exposes the tensions between various values and norms prevalent in Swedish society, and the ambiguous character of the idea of multi-culturalism. How broad is the horizon? What values and ideas can be accepted or tolerated? These issues have introduced into the debate a wider discussion on the role of religion in society, and have shown that the narrow definition of religion taken more or less for granted in Swedish policy is problematic. Can religion really be an entirely private matter?

Changes in the political party arena beg the question of whether separate confessional schools will lead to segregated communities. The xenophobic party Ny Demokrati, characterized by a relatively negative evaluation of Islam and the Muslim presence, lost votes and seats in Parliament after only one electoral term (1991–94). Other more explicitly anti-Islamic political groups have not got enough votes to come even near to representation in the Parliament.

A field where the problem of 'belonging' comes into focus is that of education. The Swedish school system has a low level of tolerance for independent or private schools. Such schools are few, and their curricula and how they are run are controlled by the authorities according to strict criteria, with close scrutiny of the norms and values imparted to pupils. All schools, even private ones, have to conform to notions of gender equality, democratic values, the rejection of racism and the upholding of human rights (as defined by international declarations and conventions), including equal status regardless of religious affiliation. This renders the question of confessional schools – Christian or Muslim – controversial, especially since these schools are seen by many as contravening the notion of integration and mainstreaming.

Instead, critics argue, such schools can lead to the creation of segregated communities. There are some functioning Muslim schools in the country; others were set up but failed after a period of time, due to a lack of funds or failure to fulfil the prerequisites of the official regulations, or sometimes due to a lack of pupils (the parents preferring to use the state school system).[23] It is important to note that a very small proportion of Muslims in Sweden make use of or are interested in confessional schools for their children, or demand them. Most are more interested in an education that will give their children the best career opportunities in the future.

On the other hand, the Christian Democratic Party (Krist-demokraterna) has achieved a stronger position (about 10 per cent of the electorate in 2002), and due to its parliamentary representation, has been able to introduce a programmatic change in the directives of the school system. In the previous directives it was stated that 'the school ... has to develop such qualities among the pupils which can support and strengthen the principles of democracy, such as tolerance, cooperation and equal rights between human beings' (Läroplan för grundskolan/Directives for Education in Primary and Secondary Schools, 1980).

This formulation, which received considerable support among the public and teachers alike, was substituted in the 1995 directives, under the influence of the Christian Democratic Party, by the following formula: 'the pupils shall be educated ... in accordance with the ethic that has been administered by Christian tradition and Western humanism'. It appears that this declaration, however, has not influenced the actual curricula of the schools in any conceivable way. At the same time, it has not found much support among teachers, nor has it been used as an argument for separate confessional schools. The leading personalities in the Christian Democratic Party deny that the formula should be regarded as directed against Islam in any way, a denial that has, however, been not entirely convincing.

Political Islam or Politically Conscious Muslims?

The welfare system came under considerable pressure during the economic crisis of the 1980s and 1990s. Consequently, social and economic conditions for certain strata deteriorated and separatist tendencies emerged. Immigrant families in the suburbs of the larger cities experiencing a high level of unemployment witnessed their children's school performances deteriorating. Social problems such as ethnic tension, increasing gang activity, violence and a high incidence of crime abounded. In a much cited book on Islam in Europe,[24] the Swedish diplomat Ingmar Karlsson has pointed out the danger of the situation in the suburbs: marginalized youth, with insufficient language competence and education, and with limited options in the labour market, constitute a potential recruitment basis not only for gang criminality, but also for political or religious extremism.

However, whereas criminal or semi-criminal gangs and ethnic tensions are indeed increasing, there is very little engagement with religious extremism or any distinct manifestation of even a moderate and non-violent political Islam. The mosques develop spheres of activities other than those that can support such tendencies.[25] On the other hand, some individuals and small groups have had contacts with radical Islamism, in the sense of religiously legitimated extremist violence, in other parts of the world. At the most, it could be argued that Sweden became a haven for some activities of that kind for a time, but with very little impact on Muslims living in the country. In other words, Sweden was used as a safe haven for Islamists, but was not regarded as a target in itself. These groups, therefore, would not have integrated into the Muslim community in Sweden and thus have no palpable impact – socially or politically.

Tensions between diverse value systems have less to do with religious affiliation and more with the differences between secular welfare state notions and the norms inherent to patriarchal tribal societies. The latter includes the social dynamics of extended families often combined with what could be referred to as the Mediterranean concept of honour and gender relations, where influence and male authority are linked to female sexual behaviour.[26] This problem has come to the fore as a consequence of the murder of Fadime Sahindal (discussed above).

Unlike the debate in the United Kingdom where the question of political Islam has been linked to demands for a separate judicial status for Muslims (such as the application of separate personal status laws for the Muslim society), there has been little of that in Sweden. As with any other aspect of Swedish legislation, family law and the laws of inheritance are secularized. In 1999, however, heated discussions on this matter took place. In his capacity as a spokesman of an umbrella council (Islamiska samarbetsrådet) of some of the officially recognized Muslim organizations, Mahmoud Aldebe[27] argued in an interview that shari'a law in matters concerning the family and inheritance should be permitted.[28] His view was that this was as much a question of religious freedom as the building of mosques. The debate (featured in some newspapers, radio and television in both Sweden and Denmark) provoked much discussion.

This begs the question of how to define religious freedom. In 1951, Sweden legislated changes in the definition of religious affiliation. Until then, every citizen had to belong to a religious community recognized by the state. From 1951 onwards, this ceased to be the case. This meant that religious affiliation was no longer registered and had no consequence whatsoever for judicial matters. The same laws apply to everyone, at least in principle. The law meant that one could be without any religious affiliation, and that the authorities had no right to demand a declaration on this. Hence, in practice, religious freedom was meant to refer to freedom of belief, freedom of worship and freedom of practice (in so far as that was due to individual free choice).

Thus, religious leaders (however defined) have no jurisdiction over members of their communities, and religious laws are not to be taken into consideration by the courts. A collective freedom of religion (freedom for communities) thus substituted for the concept of individual religious freedom, the opposite of a *millet* system[29] that is, the administrative system that was once in force in the Ottoman Empire, where each religiously defined group had a degree of legal autonomy, especially with regard to personal laws.

Hence, Aldebe's proposal contradicted the very framework of the Swedish legal system. If any part of it, for instance family law, should again be determined by religious affiliation, this would be regarded as an infringement of the individual's rights in religious matters. The definition of 'religion' and 'religious freedom' would also have to revert to a collective one, rather than the current individual one. What was therefore suggested in the debate, as a realistic compromise, was to have some kind of counselling, or advisory, 'shari'a board', responsible for advising believers – in so far as that was required – but without any legal authority or jurisdiction.

It is interesting to note that this would be a parallel to how a canon law court functions within the Catholic Church in Sweden. When the idea of shari'a courts was again put forward in a TV programme,[30] there were protests from many Muslim intellectuals, writers, professionals and active members of political parties. A Muslim member of parliament, who had reacted very negatively to Aldebe's proposal from its inception, strongly protested in a radio interview against what she regarded as outmoded patriarchal notions with no Islamic legitimacy. The protests from secular and Muslim intellectuals, and members of political parties, focused in particular on the idea of segregation: the existence of separate legal entities based on religious affiliation and against the fact that specific (conservative) religious leaders thus claim to be representatives and spokespersons for all Muslims in Sweden.

The publication, with government support, of a new Swedish translation (or rather, paraphrase or interpretation) of the Qur'an, by the retired Swedish diplomat Mohammed Knut Bernström, in 1998,[31] is considered seminal in the development of a specifically Swedish Islam. The character of this interpretation differs significantly from earlier translations by Swedish Orientalists based on strictly linguistic-historical-critical criteria. The most influential of these earlier translations was made by the Uppsala University professor of Semitic languages K.V. Zetterstéen (published in 1917 and still available in reprints). Zetterstéen's aim was to present a translation of the meaning that the Arabic text might have had in the *Hijaz* (currently Saudi Arabian) environment in the seventh century, during the time of the Prophet. By contrast, Bernström aimed to present, not what the text meant, but what it means, that is what the meaning of the text implies for a Muslim living in Sweden today.

Bernström's is a seminal work, with the text, alongside the inter-pretation-translation, and a revised Swedish commentary based on the one by Muhammad Azad.[32] It has also been scrutinized by a group working with the approval of the al-Azhar Islamic University in Cairo, which means that it has official Islamic recognition. Even more significant is how the translation has been received in Muslim circles in Sweden, which (with a few exceptions) has generally been very positive. There are several reasons for this: the Swedish literary style is of a high quality, the translator is himself a believer and practising Muslim, and, as a retired Swedish ambassador, occupies a high social standing.

The fact that the government subsidized the printing of this document indicates that it was seen as a legitimate and accepted part of the process of social integration. In addition, its publication by a renowned publisher was seen as a further seal of approval. Bernström has searched for what is relevant to Swedish society and facilitated a 'modernist' interpretation, compatible with the actual function of religions in a contemporary European society. This signals an important trend for the future.

In Conclusion

Sweden today constitutes a society in the throes of change, becoming more and more integrated into the European Union. This includes the dynamics not only of political relations with the Muslim world, but also with the Muslims living in Sweden. Sweden became an active part in the Barcelona Process in the 1990s with its stress on cooperation between the EU and the non-European regions of the Mediterranean. Old contacts are symbolized by archaeological findings and the alliance between Sweden and Turkey in the eighteenth century. With this continuity and subsequent motivation in mind, there are also important changes in Swedish society which are directly connected to the immigration of Muslims into this previously largely homogeneous country. This influx occurred in two waves: labour force immigration in the 1960s and 1970s, and refugees in the 1980s and 1990s, the latter coinciding with fluctuations in the Swedish economy, which led, in turn, to social tensions.

The development of a welfare state in the second half of the twentieth century meant a change in family structures and religious groups and institutions, whereby the secular state structures and the municipalities became the main 'security networks' for the individual. This meant the privatization of religion and the development of individualistic norms, in contrast to collective social ones. Religion thus lost much of its previously existing economic and social functions.

This secularization and privatization process was evidenced among Muslim groups in Sweden too, rendering the idea of 'religion' as an order of society less applicable, and in fact irrelevant. As a parallel development, an interest in personal religious experience and an increase in the relevance of Sufi piety emerge. To this comes a change in the availability of 'religious entertainment', that is the consumption of religious features from satellite TV, videos, tapes and (for the younger generation) the Internet, diminishing the role and authority of local religious spokesmen and leaders.

Some tensions with the government have also emerged, due *inter alia* to the breakdown of the link between religion and the traditional patriarchal tribal social structures. Young people no longer accept the customary tribal norms and codes of behaviour, but frequently search for support in reinterpretations of the religious tradition and its sources, for the integration into modern society and for the individualistic, personal choice of lifestyle (religious or secular) within the welfare state structure of Sweden.

The younger generation will continue to take part in the discussion on Swedish policy vis-à-vis world events, the Israeli–Palestinian conflict, the war in Afghanistan, and so on. But perhaps more significantly Muslim youth are substantially engaged in debates on environmental questions and in cultural activities such as literature, film and music. The general trend among active Muslim individuals and groups has been to stress their solidarity with Swedish society and to be a part of ongoing and broadly relevant social debates.

This effectively makes Islamism (as a religious diktat for the order of society or state) less appealing or even necessary. This underlines the powerful symbolism of the state-supported and socially endorsed Quranic translation-cum-interpretation, which would be frowned on by Islamist groups – whether moderate or radical. But Islamist thought is not likely to influence Swedish Muslims, as long as a strong desire for integration persists and the Swedish polity renders itself open to diversity and challenge.

Notes

1. The documentation of the conference is published by the Swedish Institute (Euro-Islam, Stockholm, 15–17 June 1995).
2. The documentation likewise published by the Swedish Institute (The Second Conference on Euro-Islam. Relations between the Muslim World and Europe, Mafraq, H.K. Jordan, 10–13 June 1996).

3. Swedish Foreign Ministry Report Ds (1999: 63: 121–5).
4. For a brief historical survey of these earlier relations, see Hjärpe (1998: 65–70).
5. Hjärpe (1997b: 115–22).
6. 'Det svenska studiet av islam' [The Swedish study of Islam], in Magnus Berg and Veronica Trépagny (eds.). *I andra länder: Historiska perspektiv på svensk förmedling av det främmande. En antologi* [In Other countries. Historical perspectives on the Swedish Transition of the foreign: An Anthology] (Lund, 1999), pp. 35–46.
7. Hjarpe (1994: 18–28).
8. Hjarpe (1999b: 111–20).
9. For the history of the Tatars in Finland and Sweden, see Soukkan (1985: 84–119). For an analysis of the role of their presence, see Otterbeck (1998: 145–53).
10. Of particular interest here is research on the status of 'Muslims' undertaken by Hvidtfelt (1998).
11. Sander (1997: 179–210).
12. For an example of empirical research on these differences, see Koctürk-Runefors (1991).
13. For a discussion on the relation between the actual functioning of society and the norm systems, see Hjärpe (1997a: 52–69).
14. For a comprehensive survey of the Muslim organizations, communities and organized activities in Sweden, see I. Svanberg and D. Westerlund (eds.), *Blågul Islam: Muslimer i Sverige*, (Stockholm: Nora, 1999), especially pp. 14–139. Cf. the continuing account in the annual report given by the SST, Samarbetsnämnden för statsbidrag till trossamfund (The Cooperation Board for Governmental Support of Religious Communities).
15. An early example is the very revealing interview with the Imam Faruk Celebi in Stockholm, in Richert, Unge and Wagner (1985: 195–9).
16 'Blågul islam', blue-and-yellow Islam, the appellation alludes to the colours of the Swedish flag.
17. Otterbeck (2000b). See also Otterbeck (2000a: 247–66).
18. The Islamic Information Association.
19. Ouis (1999: 235–48).
20. Other participants with academic credentials and both practising and/or religiously engaged, include Pierre Durrani, Assistant Professor of History of Religions, specializing in Islamology, and Anne Sofie Roald.
21. A list of home page addresses can be found in Stenberg (1999: 128).
22. Gerle (1999).
23. Quoted from Johansson (1999: 175–94).
24. Karlsson (1994). The book is available in both a Turkish and an Arabic translation.
25. As quoted in Karlsson (1999: 195–212).
26. Quoted from Koctürk-Runefors (1991: 125 and 191).
27. Aldebe was also very engaged in the Islamiska informationsföreningen.
28. Some of the debate is referred to in *Svenska Dagbladet*, 17 September 1999. The newspaper *Dagen* (connected with Pentecostals and other evangelical movements) took up the question in a rather controversial way, and it was also taken up by the Danish press.
29. The matter is discussed in a doctoral dissertation by Alwall (1998).

30. *Fittja Paradiso*, a TV programme set in a suburban environment, and with a very high degree of immigrant participation.
31. *Koranens budskap i svensk tolkning av Mohammed Knut Bernström med kommentarer av Muhammad Azad* (The message of the Qur'an in Swedish interpretation by Mohammed Knut Bernström and comments by Muhammad Azad) (Stockholm, 1998).
32. A presentation of the very interesting personality of Muhammad Azad is to be found in the Saudi magazine *Aramco World* (Houston, Texas: Aramco Services Company), January/February 2002, pp. 6–32.

References

Alwall, Jonas. *Muslim Rights and Plights: The Religious Liberty Situation of a Minority in Sweden*, (Lund, 1998).

Berqvist, Jenny. 'Gröna svar på gröna frågor, Muslimskt miljöengagemang' [Green answers to green questions. Muslim engagement in environmental issues], in *Svensk Religionshistorisk Årsskrift* (Swedish Annual of History of Religions), 1999, pp. 196–216.

Gerle, Elisabeth. *Mångkulturalism – för vem?* [Cultural pluralism – for whom?] (Stockholm: Nora, 1999).

Hjärpe, Jan. 'Meeting with Islam', in *Meeting Foreign Cultures* (Scripta Minora Regiae Societatis Humanorum Litterarum Lundensis, 1994).

——. 'Some Problems in the Meeting between European and Islamic Legal Traditions. Examples from the Human Rights Discussion', in Tuuli Forsgren and Martin Peterson (eds.). *Cultural Crossroads in Europe* (Stockholm: FRN, 1997a), pp. 52–69.

——. 'Historiography and Islamic Vocabulary in War and Peace: A Memento for Conflict Resolution in the Muslim World', in D.P. Fry and K. Björkqvist (eds.). *Cultural Variation in Conflict Resolution: Alternatives to Violence* (New Jersey: Mahwah, 1997b).

——.'Islam and Scandinavia. The Problem of Religious Influence', in Elisabeth Piltz (ed.). *Byzantium and Islam in Scandinavia. Compilations from a Symposium at Uppsala University, 15–16 June 1996* (Jonsered, 1998).

——. 'Det svenska studiet av islam' [The Swedish study of Islam], in Magnus Berg and Veronica Trépagny (eds.). *I andra länder: Historiska perspektiv på svensk förmedling av det främmande, En antologi* [In Other Countries. Historical Perspectives on Swedish Transition of the Foreign. An Anthology] (Lund, 1999a).

——. 'Revolution in Religion: From Medievalism to Modernity and Globalization', in Göran Therborn (ed.). *Globalization and Modernities – Experiences and Perspectives of Europe and Latin America* (Stockholm: FRN, 1999b).

Hvidtfelt, Håkan. 'Den muslimska faran – om mediebilden av Islam' [The Muslim danger – on the picture of Islam in the media], in Y. Brune (ed.). *Mörk magi i vita medier.Svensk nyhetsjournalistik om invandrare, flyktingar och rasism* [Dark Magic in White Media. Swedish Journalism on Immigrants] (Stockholm, 1998).

Johansson, Bo. 'Islamiska friskolor – lyckad integration eller hot mot mångfalden?' [Islamic free schools – succesful integration or a threat against pluralism?], in *Blågul islam* [Blue and Yellow Islam], 1999, pp. 175–94.

Karlsson, Ingmar. *Islam och Europa: Samlevnad eller konfrontation* [Islam and Europe: Coexistence or confrontation?] (Stockholm: Wahlström, 1994).
Karlsson, Pai. 'Islam tar plats – moskéer och deras function' [Islam takes a place – mosques and their functions'], in *Blågul Islam* [Blue and Yellow Islam], 1999.
Koctürk-Runefors, Tahire. *En fråga om heder. Turkiska kvinnor hemma och utomlands* [A Question of Honour. Turkish women at home and abroad] (Stockholm, 1991).
Koranens budskap i svensk tolkning av Mohammed Knut Bernström med kommentarer av Muhammad Asad [The Message of the Qur'an in Swedish Interpretation by Mohammed Knut Bernström and Comments by Muhammad Azad], (Stockholm, 1998).
Otterbeck, Jonas. 'The Baltic Tatars – the First Muslim Group in Modern Sweden', in Karin Junefelt and Martin Peterson (eds.). *Cultural Encounters in East Central Europe* (Stockholm: FRN, 1998), pp. 145–53.
——. 'Local Islamic Universalism: Analyses of an Islamic Journal in Sweden', in Felice Dassetto (ed.). *Paroles d'Islam: Individus, sociétés et discours dans l'islam européen contemporain* (Paris: Maisonneuve & Larose, 2000a), pp. 247–66.
——. 'Islam på svenska. Tidskriften Salaam och islams globalisering' [Islam in Swedish: The magazine Salaam and the globalization of Islam], in *Lund Studies in the History of Religions*, Vol. 11 (Lund, 2000b).
Ouis, Pernilla. 'Islamisk ekoteologi – en ny grön rörelse?' [Islamic ecotheology – a new 'green' movement?], in *Blågul islam*, 1999, pp. 235–48.
Richert, Annika, Suzanne Unge and Ulla Wagner, (eds.). *Islam: Religion, Kultur, Samhälle* [Islam: Religion, Culture, Society] (Stockholm, 1985), pp. 195–9.
Sander, Åke. 'To What Extent is the Swedish Muslim Religious?', in S. Vertovec and C. Peach (eds.). *Islam in Europe. The Politics of Religion and Community* (London: Macmillan, 1997), pp. 179–210.
Soukkan, Türker. 'Ett tatariskt lokalsamhälle i Sverige. En minoritetsgrupp i ett brett tidsperspektiv' [A Tatar society in Sweden. A minority group in a broad temporal perspective], in *Svenska Forskningsinstitutet i Istanbul. Meddelanden*, October 1985, pp. 84–119.
Stenberg, Leif. *Muslim i Sverige – lära och liv* [Muslims in Sweden – Doctrine and Life] (Stockholm, 1995).
Svanberg, Ingvar and Westerlund, David (eds.). *Blågul islam. Muslimer i Sverige* [Bue and Yellow Islam. Muslims in Sweden] (Stockholm: Nora, 1999).
Swedish Foreign Ministry Report Ds 1999:63. *Tradition och förnyelse: En studie av Nordafrika och Mellanöstern* [Tradition and Innovation: A Study on North Africa and the Middle East] (Stockholm, 1999) pp. 121–5.
Widstrand, Pai, K. 'Islam tar plats – moskéer och deras funktion' [Islam takes a place – mosques and their functions], in *Blågul islam*, 1999, pp. 195–212.

Newspapers and Magazines

Dagen (Stockholm)
Svenska Dagbladet (Stockholm)
Saudi Aramco World (Aramco Services Company, Houston, Texas), January/February 2002, pp. 6–32

4
Islam: An Alternative Globalism and Reflections on the Netherlands[1]

Jan Nederveen Pieterse

Historical and cultural differences within Islam are so considerable that the category 'Islam', with its unitary ring and homogenizing aura, may need to be put in quotation marks. Like Christianity, Islam is a term that works at a certain distance: at close range, finer distinctions are necessary. Of course, there is a common core to the diverse expressions of Islam, but what is at the core, its size and halo varies considerably. The collective self-awareness that identifies and proclaims the existence of Islam is not unproblematic.

Further, to what extent is it justified to call immigrants from Muslim countries 'Muslims'? They may be categorized that way by administrative and clerical authorities and scholars of Islam in the countries of origin and residence, and this obviously serves the interests of discursive and administrative neatness. But to what extent is Islam central to the lives of immigrants from Muslim countries? There may be a difference between 'cultural' and 'religious' Muslims. For some, Islam may be part of what they have moved away from. Besides the circuit of mosque communities – the focus of this chapter – there is the circuit of coffee-houses, and in addition there may be those who frequent neither. This is a point of caution before stepping into the argument: the status of Islam is not to be taken for granted; the statistics are to be taken in quotation marks and their significance is not obvious.

The relationship between the global and the local has been one of recurrent tension in Islam. Islam has a universalist vocation, but no single organizational structure. Islam is a form of globalism, but is organized only in local structures. Islam is a holistic religion, an ideology of total alignment between religion and politics, society and state, but it survives and is revitalized amidst the process of differentiation which is a feature of complex societies.

For centuries Islam has spread world-wide carrying a universalist vocation, as part of the historical momentum of globalization. What then is the place of Islam in contemporary globalization? According to Hassan al-Turabi, the leading ideologue of the Muslim Brotherhood of Sudan: 'if pan-Islam is partly an outcome of the increasing internationalization of human life, it would also give an impetus to that momentum' (1993: 18). The Muslim diaspora, like other diasporas, may be viewed as part of the development of a global civil society: yet, how does this chime with the holistic claims of Islam? Will the Muslim diaspora merge with the host societies and generate new, hybrid forms? Will Islam 'secularize' overseas if it is exposed to the same influences that have led to the depopulation of Christian churches – the impact of urbanization, education, national media, in addition to the process of acculturation? In Asia and Africa, Islam has generated new forms and articulations: what will be the course of Islam in the West?

Migration is induced by global differentiation and at the same time an attempt to cushion and negotiate its impact. The question considered here is migration/refiguration, or how does Islam change in the process of migration? One of the fallacies in thinking about cultural difference is the reification of difference and viewing it in static terms. Both immigrants and host cultures tend to be represented (except the young of the second generation) with a peculiar emphasis on their unchanging cultural characteristics. This is odd, if only because migration is a travel experience and in most cultures travel is one of the central metaphors of change. Or can migration also be viewed as a process of cultural conservation and reconstruction?

The first section of this chapter is a note on internal migration while the second reflects the changing political economy of overseas migration. The third section is concerned with travelling Islam and compares the impact of internal and overseas migration. Section four deals with patterns of intercultural cohabitation which are shaped by the historical treatment of cultural differences in societies, reflected in legislation and ideological orientations: it is within these vortexes that immigrant culture is reconstructed. For instance, there are distinct differences between multiculturalism in Britain and pillarization in the Netherlands, but both have in common that they define immigrant groups in terms of 'ethnicity' rather than 'religion'. Section five is concerned with the boundaries that mark cultural identities, which can be talked about either in static or fluid terms. The rise and decline of boundaries is one way of looking at the encoding and decoding of identity constructions: do enclave cultures persist or are hybrid identities emerging?

Migration/Urbanization

Internal migration and urbanization mean leaving village life behind and entering a complex, differentiated social world. In the urban centres one's social world and religious community no longer coincide, as in village Islam. Religion, according to Schiffauer (1988), becomes privatized, optional, no more than a segment of life. Not all migrants adhere or turn to Islam, nor does it carry the same meaning for those who do. The overall relationship between religion and society changes. If society is primarily defined as secular – as in Turkey – the religious community becomes a counterweight to secular society, and the relationship becomes one not of complementarity but of opposition; Islamic discourse can thus become a vehicle of protest (Schiffauer, 1988: 152).

What induces migration from the countryside in the first place is that communal economies are unsettled as a consequence of the creeping advance of the capitalist world economy. When this occurs in conjunction with the retreat of the state from its welfare functions, as now increasingly happens in many countries, Islamic institutions may step into the void left by the state. Likewise, Islamism, or political Islam, may step into the ideological void left open by the waning appeal of the ideologies of nationalism and socialism. Where communal relations have been shattered, political Islam reinstates a moral economy that claims to reunite the community of believers. Reinvoking ideals of social justice, a politics of redistribution that is egalitarian and privileges a place for the poor, it presents a moral economy in the vernacular of tradition. But in the process tradition is being reconstructed and the circumstances have changed: under the banner of sameness, Islamic discourse has changed. Islam is being politicized in a manner different from the official 'Islam of the powerful'.

If the twin processes of integration into world capitalism and the retreat of the state are crucial conditions for the rise of political Islam and Islamism, the same may hold for religious revival movements such as Hindutva in India, and ethnic and separatist movements in other societies: vernaculars of discontent, negotiating the present by reclaiming the past. In reinvoking and reconstructing moral economies, these movements attempt to serve as a buffer against the advance of capitalism. The question is whether they can be more effective than nationalism and socialism which, each in different ways, have sought to channel or counter the impact of capitalism. Whatever the outcome, the price paid in the process is that power accrues to a wide variety of religious and ethnic entrepreneurs who give their own ideological and political inflection to this process.

What changes does Islam undergo when travelling? Initially, it may become more central and prominent in some people's lives than it used to be in the countryside. Deterritorialized from the village, Islam may show a growing orthodoxy. A tendency towards growing 'scripturalism' has been in evidence throughout Islam since the nineteenth century, as manifested in an increasing emphasis on Quranic teaching, Islamic education and building mosques (Geertz, 1968). The scripturalist tendency comes at the expense of the popular Islam of saint worship, healing, Sufism and local brotherhoods. The imam rather than the saint, marabout or sage becomes the central figure. This tendency of clericalization is reinforced in the migration process. When Islam leaves its original landscape what travels are not the marabout shrines nor the rural folk practices and brotherhoods, but the Qur'an and Quranic teaching. The turn to scriptures, while presented as an orientation to unchanging revelation and holding fast to tradition, is itself highly modern.

Besides providing shelter from the storm of economic uprooting, the mosque may serve as the university of the poor: offering orientation, basic education and a sense of historical depth. The imams are the intellectuals of the migrant working class. 'The holy text or traditions give certainty in a world of moral void; they are a sure protection against the dehumanizing impact of cynicism' (Parekh, 1993: 141).

What form this takes differs from place to place as each locality brings together a different ensemble of diverse currents. The vortex of rural/urban cohabitation shapes the local play of class and culture, of economic and political forces and ways of experiencing and viewing them through maps of meaning. Local histories of rural/urban relations, patterns of state/society relations and the local mix of regional and global influences make for different alignments in Egypt, Algeria, Turkey, Sudan or northern Nigeria. Recognizing the specific local ensemble of global influences makes for what Doreen Massey calls 'a global sense of place': 'a sense of place which is extraverted, which includes a consciousness of its links with the wider world, which integrates in a positive way the global and the local' (1993: 66).

There is no firm or stable demarcation between the global and the local because, like different kinds of dough in a marble cake, they mingle and interpenetrate. The global and the local are not merely geographical categories but also ways of seeing, optical devices and perceptual categories. A stable demarcation or contradiction between them may seem to exist only from a particular point of view, a fixed point in space and time. With a slight shift of the kaleidoscope however, the relations may change altogether: the local appears in its global aspect, the global as an assemblage of travelling local features.

Islam itself is a form of globalism, a global civilizational ethos and, as pan-Islamism, an aspiring world order (Beeley, 1992). More than the other 'religions of the book', Islamism has secularized religion in merging spiritual order and temporal power and making religion equivalent to political formation. This makes Islam particularly modern and is one reason why Islam, including contemporary political Islam, should not be viewed as an anti-modernity, as is common in many contemporary polemics, but as an alternative modernity (as stressed by Al-Azmeh, 1993). The terminology of 'fundamentalism' and the associated dichotomy between tradition and modernity are fundamentally inadequate, as I have argued elsewhere (Nederveen Pieterse, 1994). It is, rather, the modernity of political Islam which needs to be assessed. Nevertheless, Islam is at odds with the modern state and nationalism, and thus it has been argued that it has no place to accommodate modern international relations (George, 1993: 4). Yet if it is true that we have entered a post-nationalist phase, what does this mean for the possible futures of Islam?

Islam under the Shadow of the World Trade Center

In colonial times the cities in the colonies were the most internationalized. Now another kind of internationalization is occurring in the post-imperial metropolitan centres of corporate activity. The skylines of global cities have been changing under the influence of the restructuring of global capital over the past decades. In the interstices of the metropolitan centres, under the shadow of the glossy façades of mega-capitals, with a view of the changing skylines from below, an immigrant workforce installs itself. Saskia Sassen observes the presence of a migrant or immigrant workforce in the United States that is especially strong in major cities, which also have the largest concentration of corporate power. We see here an interesting correspondence between great concentrations of corporate power and concentrations of an amalgamated 'other'.

The fact that most of the people working in the corporate city during the day are low-paid secretaries, mostly women – many of them immigrant or African-American women – is not included in the representation of the corporate economy or corporate culture. And the fact that at night a whole other, mostly immigrant workforce installs itself in these spaces ... and inscribes the space with a whole different culture (manual labour, often music, lunch breaks at midnight) is an invisible event. (Sassen, 1993: 101)

Internal migration in Muslim countries was largely induced by world capitalism travelling overseas, whereas overseas migration means travelling *into* the sphere of world capitalism, seeking shelter under the shadow of the World Trade Centres.

By destroying traditional means of livelihood, and by prole-tarianizing a greater part of the population in some regions, foreign investment encourages the movement of people very often in the direction where capital is coming from. (Pellerin, 1994: 5)

On the one hand, the internationalization of economies promotes the outflow of labour and, on the other, the casualization of the labour market in global cities makes for an expansion in the supply of low-wage jobs generated by major growth sectors. This twofold process both produces new migrations and facilitates their absorption (Sassen, 1991: 316–19).

Islamism and capitalism can both be described as 'world processes' (Pred and Watts, 1992: 45) and as such they intersect in the matrix of migration. In Islam migration is commonly understood by reference to the model of the *hijrah* of the Prophet to Medina and of his followers to Abyssinia. Thus according to the imam of the London Central Mosque, migration may be described 'as a tradi-tional Islamic way of life' (Darsh, 1980: 75). He quotes a Hadith (saying of the Prophet) indicating that 'migration would not stop until repentance stopped and repentance would not stop until the sun rose in the West. The *hijrah* will continue until the Last Day.' He continues,

If we consider the different patterns of early Muslim migration, we shall discover a number of common factors between them and the present-day migrations. Some resulted from persecution, some from trading connections and others from desire for financial betterment. (Darsh, 1980: 76)

This papers over the controversy of the migration issue in Islam. An important difference in the pattern of migrations is ignored:

In some sense these communities [Muslim communities that have settled in the West] by emigrating *into* rather than *away from* the non-Muslim world, have challenged the basic Muslim concept of Muslim solidarity exemplified by Muhammad's own *hijra* from Mecca to Medina. (Christie, 1991: 459)

From a radical Islamist point of view, travelling to the West, like imitating the West, may be a form of 'westoxification' and a betrayal of Islam. For instance, in the words of an orthodox Muslim leader in Turkey, Shaykh Zahid Kotku, 'To voyage to foreign countries simply to earn more money is irresponsible' (in Mardin, 1993: 222).

Indeed, there are different ways of maintaining a core of orthodoxy within a changing world. The imam's reading of migration both accommodates and papers over the episode of world capitalism and the significance of contemporary global uneven development. In a narrative of continuity history is sidelined.

In the matrix of migration, local and global processes interpenetrate. The global standing and aspirations of Islam are locally meaningful: they inspire a sense of identity and self-worth among the Muslim diaspora; they maintain the transnational infrastructure of Islamic culture, from the *hajj* (the Muslim pilgrimage to Mecca) to subventions and donations from various quarters of Muslim influence. At the same time, global Islam is fragmented along denominational, political and ethnic lines and the awareness of global unity and momentum is simultaneously an awareness of division, conflict and dispersal. The Muslim diaspora is the counter-image to the *hajj* in Mecca, an outflow as compared to an in-gathering. In the Muslim diaspora the paradox of Islam becomes manifest: Islam is a global project that is organized only in local structures.

As a form of globalism, Islam both colludes and competes with world capitalism. The cross-cultural trade networks of the Muslim world are part of the infrastructure of world capitalism. The collusion with global capitalism generates networks of cooperation. In competition it has been on the defensive and, like capitalism itself, riven with internal contradictions. The attacks on the World Trade Center in New York, presumably by a militant Islamist group, which may be sponsored by orthodox forces in Saudi Arabia, illustrate the dramatic scope of contradictions within Islam.

While part of the outflow of investments from oil-rich Muslim countries, through the recycling of petrodollars in the 1970s, underpins the expansion of world capitalism, another part is invested in contestation with the local manifestations of global capitalism in Muslim countries. The consequences and ramifications of *infitah* (liberal) economies in Muslim countries are contested by orthodox and militant groups, who are financially and ideologically supported from the very same centres which participate in and enhance the process of capitalist expansion. This inconsistency is part of the weakness of the *pax Islamica*, which in turn reflects the inability of its moral economy to encompass world capitalism – witness the marginal character of 'Islamic economics' (Kuran, 1993).

Part of the flipside of Islam's rendezvous with global capitalism is that the negative media reporting generated by the contestation with capitalism rubs off on the Muslim diaspora. It generates and sustains a 'problem image' of Muslim minorities in the West who are thereby kept on the periphery of the social imaginary (see Hargreaves and Perotti, 1993).

Mosques without Minarets in the Netherlands

Is it possible to generalize about the experiences of migration? What is the difference between the experience of urbanization and that of overseas migration, as the deterritorialization of Islam mark II? The long-term tendency towards growing orthodoxy and 'clericalization' may be reinforced in either mode of migration. Travelling overseas, Islam may undergo further changes as well: arguably, a process of cultural differentiation or 'ethnicization' of Islam; political differentiation among and within ethnicities and nationalities; and generation differences. All of this in various ways illustrates Gramsci's observation: '[E]very religion is in reality a multiplicity of distinct and contradictory religions' (quoted in Pred and Watts, 1992: 45).

What shapes the immigrant experience and the formation of local Muslim cultures in global spaces is, first, the local pattern of intercultural cohabitation which differs from country to country, and second, the mix of transnational and cross-cultural influences which Muslims encounter. This can be looked at only in specific terms. We will examine this in the case of Muslims in the Netherlands.

Mosques without minarets are not the image of choice among Muslims. The preferred image is 'from mats to minarets' (Landman, 1992), an image that reflects the process of institutionalization of Islam (Waardenburg, 1988). In the course of 30 years, from the first labour migrations in the 1960s to the present, Muslim workers, many of them illiterates from the countryside, have brought over their families, set up enterprises, sent their children to school and have worked themselves up to establish a cultural presence. 'From mats to minarets' is a narrative of achievement and social mobility: from humble origins to proud attainment.

'Mosques without minarets' evoke a different image: of a subculture on the margins. A number of newly built mosques in the Netherlands in fact do have minarets, although most do not, as school buildings, redundant churches and synagogues, factory halls and homes are converted to serve as prayer halls. But the minarets do not tower above the surrounding buildings, do not claim central public sites, as is mostly the case in Muslim countries, especially for newly built mosques. The minarets are lower than the high-rise offices of capital, lower than the World Trade Centres, lower even than the apartment high-rises among which they nestle – proud yet modest, substantial yet, to outsiders, barely noticeable. In a different way the place and function of church buildings have changed: long gone are the days of *ecclesia triumphans* when churches were the dominant structures in the cityscapes. Gone too are the days when churches in height and location competed only with the town halls. Now banks and office towers on the model of the World Trade Center architecturally and spatially dominate cityscapes.

There is the further difference between the migration of Islam to the East and to the West. To Asia and Africa, Muslims came as traders and at a time when Islam was in the ascendant. Their settlements often formed separate quarters within towns where they sometimes enjoyed a separate legal status as trading minorities. To the West, however, Muslims came as workers at a time when global Islam was on the defensive.

In the West, minarets may be controversial markers of cultural presence. If the presence of immigrants in the corporate city centres is marginal, little noticed or invisible, the immigrant presence in neighbourhoods may be highly visible. Reflecting on the reactions to the construction of a minaret in Dalston in the northeast London borough of Hackney, Gilsenan observes:

> Imagine – and it is very difficult for those who have not experienced the world of the colonized – the effect that outside forces, over a relatively short period of time, can have on the transformation of the *whole* of the relations that make up urban space, including its sacred geography and unquestioned givens of the way things are in cities. Imagine, not only one building being constructed on an alien model, but an entire system of urban life in its economic, political, and symbolic-cultural forms being imposed upon already existing towns and cities that have been organized on quite different bases. (Gilsenan, 1982: 195)

In the Netherlands the main groups of Muslims are Turks, Moroccans and Surinamese. These reflect different migration histories: colonial migration for the Surinamese and labour migration for the Turks and Moroccans. Colonial migration is multi-class and involves greater familiarity with and a greater degree of integration into the metropolitan culture, in terms of language, education and jobs. The Surinamese are more integrated in Dutch society and, on the whole, rank higher on the ethnic status hierarchy than Turks and Moroccans. Over time the composition of migration flows has changed: family reunification brought a greater number of women. The migration of refugees and dissidents reflects economic and political instability in the countries of origin, as well as the closing off of labour migration in Western Europe. Asylum-seekers often break ties with their country of origin and thus stand in a different relationship to the community centres in which the culture of origin is reconstructed. Immigrants are further differentiated, of course, according to their regional origin, time of migration, which generation of immigration they belong to, political and religious affiliation, level of education and employment.

The numbers of Muslim immigrants are modest in the Netherlands compared to Britain (with a much more differentiated South Asian component) and France (with a greater North African and Middle Eastern presence). The largest group are the Turks, estimated in 1991 to be between 200,000 and 220,000; the Moroccans number approximately 150,000; and the Surinamese Muslims 22,000. They are mainly concentrated in the four largest cities (Amsterdam, Rotterdam, The Hague, Utrecht) where, in 1991, they constituted on average 13.4 per cent of the total population, with the highest concentration in Amsterdam (15.5 per cent). In Amsterdam in 1991 the total number of inhabitants was 702,731, of whom 108,861 were aliens, including Turkish citizens (24,128), Moroccan citizens (33,902) and Surinamese citizens (6,004). If we include Dutch citizens of Surinamese and Antillean ethnic origin, the percentage of inhabitants of alien origin is 24.3 per cent of the total city population (van Amersfoort 1992: 444). In other words, a quarter of the inhabitants of Amsterdam are of 'alien' origin, of which roughly a third are Turks and Moroccans.

What is being carried along the routes of labour migration is not a sophisticated form of Quranic teaching. As the imam of the London Central Mosque notes, 'most of the imams in this country lack the basic training required to lead the prayer in a village mosque, not to mention in a place of worship in a more sophisticated and intellectually superior society' (Darsh, 1980: 89), and this applies more generally. For the first generation of immigrants who came to Western Europe as 'guest-workers' in times of economic boom and who on the whole occupy a weak socio-economic position, Islam serves as a form of cultural identification and belonging:

Most of the Muslim groups here feel at home when they get an Imam who is from the same village or area as the one from which they themselves came and who speaks the same language as they do and who is capable of reciting or reading a few chapters of the Holy Qu'ran. (Darsh, 1980: 89)

It follows that Islam is broken down in cultural units – Moroccan, Turkish, Surinamese, Pakistani, Moluccan, etc. Considering that the nationhood of others is often classified as 'ethnicity', this means that many Muslims are categorized in those terms. This clashes with 'a key principle of Islam that religious identity should prevail over ethnic identity' (Christie, 1991: 457). On the one hand, the *Umma* (Islamic nation) seems to be reconfirmed in the Muslim diaspora, while, on the other, it is broken up by national and cultural differences.

There are many different nodes to the Islamic world network and each locality brings together a different ensemble of diverse currents. A brief overview of mosque communities in the Netherlands and their cultural, national, ethnic and political diversities may illustrate the mix of global/local influences and the way the

Muslim diaspora is implicated in the vicissitudes of transnational politics and political economy.

Among Turkish Muslims the main organization is the Netherlands Islamic Foundation (Hollanda Diyanet Vakfi) which answers to the governmental Directorate for Religious Affairs in Ankara. This subsidizes the construction and upkeep of mosques and brings over imams schooled in Turkey. Presently, it owns approximately 150 mosques and rents another ten. The aim of this government involvement is to control the growth of orthodox and Islamist groups in Europe, presumably because it could affect the political situation in Turkey. The head of the organization in The Hague is seated under a portrait of Kemal Atatürk. For several years the world Muslim organization Rabita (Rabitat al-Alam al-Islami) in Mecca funded the Turkish imams sent to the Netherlands, but on condition that they preach in Arabic. Since 1986 Turkey has paid for the imams (Waardenburg, 1988).

One of the competing organizations among Muslim Turks in Western Europe has been the Teblighi movement led by Cemalettin Kaplan in Cologne, also known as the 'Khomeini of Cologne'. With funding from Iran shrinking, the mosques associated with Kaplan decreased as well (down to three in 1989): the funds to keep mosques and imams going were simply lacking. Another orthodox Turkish association is Milli Görüscu (National Vision), which runs some 15 mosques throughout the country (Beunders and Huygen, 1989).

In 1989 there were some 250 mosques in the Netherlands, 100 of which are Moroccan (Sijtsma, 1989: 150). The Moroccan government also exercises influence over Moroccan mosques but without the tight organization of the Turkish government and without providing funding. The Union of Moroccan Mosques in the Netherlands (UMMON) and Amicales are influential government arms, but the mosques are run by local foundations. Moroccans in the Netherlands hail mainly from the Rif mountains and from the south, rural populations who are newcomers to orthodoxy and among whom regional divisions play a large part.

Some years ago a few Moroccan mosques turned for funding to the Islamic Call Society in Libya, founded by Gadaffi in 1972, a loose organization which seeks to merge Islam with Gadaffi's Green Book ideas of socialism and women's emancipation. In order to suppress Moroccan infighting this organization sent Libyan and Filipino imams to the Netherlands.

Surinamese and South Asian Muslims are organized in the World Islamic Mission, which controls some 42 mosques for Surinamese, Pakistanis and Indians, united by Urdu as a common language. Established in 1976, the Mission is affiliated with the Muslim World Congress headquartered in Karachi. Affiliated with the Mission are the large mosques in the Bijlmer (a suburb of dormitory high-rises constructed in the 1970s in the south-east of Amsterdam which houses many immigrants) and Utrecht, which were originally established with funding from Saudi Arabia and other Arabic states. Surinamese Muslims further maintain an Islamic parliament headquartered in Arnhem and the Aqaidul Islam organization in The Hague.

There are many other Muslim organizations active in the Netherlands such as the Ahmaddiya movement, the Süleymanci group and several Sufi orders. Attempts to establish a federation of Muslim organizations, a central Muslim council and umbrella institutions such as Islamic broadcasting have repeatedly failed. Instead, there is a coming and going of organizations, councils and federations unevenly funded from various quarters, including Saudi Arabia, Kuwait and Libya.

Establishing Muslim institutions is also a form of transnational fundraising and job creation, a way to establish lucrative links with oil-rich Muslim countries. According to the imam of the London Central Mosque: 'In one small area with a population of approximately 3,000 people, I counted no less than six Muslim societies' (as quoted in Darsh, 1980: 80). It shows the scattered infrastructure of global Islam: one Mecca, many centres. This also points to the structure of Islamism: the lack of a central unit.

The relationship between home government control and government financial means affects the scope for autonomy: Turkey exercises greater influence over its Muslim diaspora in the name of Kemal Atatürk than Morocco does over Moroccan Muslims in the name of King Hassan II. Fluctuating oil revenues may affect the degree of orthodoxy and the ebb and flow of 'fundamentalism', or Islamism.

Local encounters such as between Surinamese and South Asian Muslims in the Netherlands (typically in the port city of Rotterdam[2]) make for new formations, such as the World Islamic Mission. Overseas colonial history informs local cultural mixing: thus the Lalla Rookh organization in Utrecht serves as a meeting place for Surinamese Muslims and Hindus. Islam is preached in the Netherlands in several languages: Turkish, Arabic, Urdu, English and Dutch, three of which are transnational. Travelling Islam is intercultural Islam, much more so than in its countries of origin.

The Amsterdam skyline is lower than that of New York, London or Paris, but there is a concentration of multinational capital around the World Trade Centre, which is part of the southern axis of corporate construction extending toward Schiphol airport. Another area of corporate concentration is the teleport at the northern axis of the city (*Boomtown*, 1988). It is in the interstices of the edifices of mega-capital that immigrant labour finds a niche. In sweatshops, particularly in the garment industry, the immigrant workforce delivers the goods for just-in-time capitalism. Turkish-owned sweatshops form an important infrastructure of the Amsterdam garment industry.

Unemployment among the Moroccan and Turkish immigrants is high and their level of schooling is low. 'The vanguard which has managed to find a paying job either does the same work as the first generation or works for their own ethnic group in jobs in which vertical mobility is virtually lacking' (Aboutaleb and van der Burght, 1986: 189).

The spatial locations of the mosques differ: Turkish mosques are often centrally located in cities and then in neighbourhoods; Moroccan mosques are typically found in low-income city neighbourhoods; Surinamese/South Asian mosques in low-income suburbs or neighbourhoods; and smaller communities in rural towns such as the Moluccan Muslims with their mosque in Ridderkerk (Slomp, 1984).

Vortexes of Cohabitation

The Netherlands is a relatively open country with a higher degree of international interdependence than its neighbours. A much higher percentage of Dutch GNP is generated abroad, through trade, services and investments, than in neighbouring countries. This openness goes back a long way in Dutch history. From the twelfth century onwards the Low Countries developed a special niche in the region in which they competed with their neighbours on the basis of openness as a selling point. By deliberate strategy, merchants and nobles combined in imposing no limitations on trade with foreigners and non-Christians, setting low tolls and permitting the right of return of cargo and ships in time of war. Elsewhere, I have termed this the political economy of tolerance (Nederveen Pieterse, 1983). This also found expression in cultural orientations, such as the fifteenth-century saying, in defiance of Spanish-Habsburg Catholic domination, 'better Turkish than Popish'. It found expression in welcoming religious and political dissidents and persecuted minorities from abroad – Sephardic Jews from Portugal and Spain, Huguenots from France, Pilgrims from England – who through their skills and networks contributed enormously to the Dutch economy. For the Dutch, 'tolerated' minorities have historically been *traits d'union* to the world economy.

In England, the head of state is also the head of the Church of England; other denominations have a less privileged status. English legislation does not take account of Islam: the blasphemy law does not apply to Islam, and ritual slaughter, polygamous marriage and female circumcision are not recognized. Muslims are treated as ethnic minorities under statutes derived from Human Rights conventions. Religious institutions receive no general support from the state, but can be recognized as charities and granted tax exemptions: in 1985, 329 mosques were thus recognized (Rath, Groenendijk and Penninx, 1991: 106–8).

In the Netherlands since the constitution of the early nineteenth century the principle of equality of religions has been constitutionally anchored. Equal rights in terms of state support for education were granted to Catholics only in 1917. The financing of schools founded by religious organizations established the system of 'pillarization', also known as the 'silver strings' between the state and Christian denominations. In the revised constitution of 1983 the principle of equality was extended to non-religious convictions. Islam is placed on the same footing as Jewish, Hindu or Humanist groups. The blasphemy law also applies to Islam and days off for Islamic holidays are recognized in law. In 1987 the same rules applying to the ringing of church bells were extended to calls to prayer from mosques. State support for establishing places of worship is a recommended policy, on the argument that religious self-organization for those who come from societies where religion plays an important part is natural. At the same time, Muslims are recognized only as 'ethnic minorities'; as a consequence those groups who are not recognized as ethnic minorities, such as Palestinians and Pakistanis, do not fall under the terms of state support (Rath, Groenendijk and Penninx, 1991: 108–11).

While 'multiculturalism' in England has been patterned on the colonial experience (Ali, 1992: 104) as the main way in which cultural difference has been recognized, 'pillarization' in the Netherlands refers to the history of cultural difference within the nation along religious lines – among Catholics, Protestants and the non-church-affiliated. Pillarization was the Dutch model of cultural pluralism from the 1910s to the 1970s.

In the 1980s there was talk of the return of pillarization with a view to immigrants. Pillarization seemed a logical mode in which to incorporate the newcomers. Thus Christian Democrats spoke of 'emancipation within one's own circle', just as 60 years earlier this applied to Catholics and Protestants who each received state subsidies for their schools and denominational institutions. There are, however, differences between denominational and multicultural pillarization. The religious pillars communicated among one another at the top; together, their elites constituted a roof over the pillarized society. But the mini-pillars of the newcomers with their low socio-economic status do not reach that high. This truncated mini-pillarization involved subsidies for immigrant institutions. The second difference was the timing: multicultural pillarization set in when religious pillarization was over, in an urbanized and secularized society in which denominational differences were becoming a thing of the past (Knippenberg and Pater, 1988).

In the course of the 1980s the pillarization model gave way to greater emphasis on integration, advocated by Social Democrats and Liberals. In the 1990s this took the form of emphasis on learning the Dutch language, courses in citizenship skills and plans for immigrant employment schemes, with a reporting system for companies.

A further dynamic is the relationship between residential patterns, employment and other indices of social participation. It has been argued that in a post-industrial welfare state such as the Netherlands this relationship has become quite weak. 'In post-industrial societies the labour market no longer appears to be the primary field of interaction determining other spheres of societal interaction. Housing, work and education have become (relative) autonomous circuits' (van Amersfoort, 1992: 439). The welfare state, and especially municipal councils in which the Labour Party predominates, as in the big cities where immigrants are concentrated, control the allocation of social housing.

In the first years of immigration, 1964–1974, unemployment among immigrants was very low. The great social problem connected with immigration was the housing situation, with overcrowded lodging houses and associated ills. The housing situation is presently more or less satisfactory, but it seems impossible to solve the unemployment problem. In the welfare state tradition, the Netherlands people ... look to the Government for a solution to social problems. But the Government has less control over the labour than over the housing market and a solution is not in sight. (van Amersfoort, 1992: 453)

Since then unemployment has been at the top of the agenda for both autochthonous and allochthonous inhabitants, i.e. those of domestic and foreign origin (with the note that those of foreign origin may be Dutch citizens if they come from the Dutch Antilles or from Surinam before 1975). For immigrants this has led to the adoption of a compulsory reporting system on companies' hiring practices, and to plans for further integration by making learning Dutch obligatory for newcomers and providing resources to make this possible.

There may also be a different way of looking at migrants and the role they play in the process of economic restructuring: '[r]ather than being a marginal mass of workers, or a specific category in the segmented market, they become a "vector" of restructuring' (Pellerin, 1994: 14). Specifically, the situation in many industrialised receiving countries allows

the coexistence of high levels of unemployment among the indigenous labour force, and economic decline more generally, with significant levels of employment amongst foreign workers, or at least some categories of foreigners. Consequently, rather than regulating economic cycles, migrants seem to participate in the deregulation of the productive process in many industries. (Pellerin, 1994: 13)

In other words, in the context of the prevailing political economic regime, there may well be a limit to minority employment schemes and to expectations for the gradual integration of immigrants in the primary labour market and society at large. The second and third generations may not find jobs, even if they have qualifications, because they are competing with indigenous white- and blue-collar sectors where unemployment has been rising and cultural capital counts. Are immigrants destined, then, to remain in cultural enclaves, as well? Cultural crossover enhances the ability of immigrants to compete in the labour market.

The Rise and Decline of Boundaries

Common understandings of the way Muslims define their boundaries with Dutch society focus on the areas of purity, sexuality and religion (Bartels, 1989). Purity relates to food (pork, *halal* meat), drink (alcohol) and habits of cleanliness. Sexuality relates to control over women. In terms of religion, Muslims may view the Netherlands as an anti-Islamic country because of its degree of secularization and the separation of church and state. Such boundaries give a sense of self-worth. Purity and sexuality provide a sense of moral superiority, which may compensate for class inferiority.

Non-Muslims construct similar boundaries of cultural difference with shifts in emphasis and meaning, focused on the suppression of women; notions of 'backwardness' – as in common comparisons, benevolent or otherwise, between immigrants and Dutch people in the past; and religion – as in ideas about Islamic orthodoxy and Islamism (Bartels, 1989). These boundaries provide Dutch people with a sense of superiority which justifies class differences. This is helpful in a society otherwise suffused with a rhetoric of egalitarianism. The cliché of Muslim suppression of women diverts attention from the marginal status of Dutch women, in a society where there is a discrepancy between a high level of feminist rhetoric and a low level of actual women's emancipation. Orthodoxy and Islamism reflect, on the one hand, popular media images of global Islam from Iran and Algeria to Bradford, and on the other, reactions to Muslim lifestyles, such as traditional dress and veiled women.

How firm and stable over time are these boundaries? To each there is an element of stretch and flexibility and in-built boundary-crossing moments. The purity boundary may be the most permeable. The higher the level of education, the more likely Muslims are to ignore dietary restrictions and integrate with Dutch society: here the same pattern prevails as in internal migration. Another effect manifests in cities with Muslim concentrations: in the marketplace cultural boundaries are increasingly being crossed. Due to recession and unemployment reducing immigrant purchasing power, ethnic entrepreneurs turn to native or cross-ethnic customers and adjust their products accordingly. Dutch retailers have long been stocking 'ethnic' produce: a fish stall which first imported fish from Spain and Portugal, then from the Caribbean, now stocks Moroccan fish. This is obvious in places such as the Albert Cuyp market, a popular, ethnically mixed food market in Amsterdam (Obbema, 1994).

The boundary of sexuality and the control of women in some respects clash with Dutch laws and customs as regards the scope of parental authority, compulsory schooling, marriage and lifestyle. Over the years there has been a series of clashes between municipal or state authorities and Muslim parents on restrictions imposed on women and daughters, reported in the popular press. Without going into detail, it is obvious that this is an unstable and conflict-ridden boundary, particularly for youngsters of the second and third generations (de Vries, 1987; Feddema, 1992).

Islam in the Netherlands is exposed to the same secularizing pressures that have eroded Dutch pillarization – education, media, urbanization. There are ample manifestations of everyday syncretism – Muslims who respect Ramadan but also buy presents and a tree at Christmas so that their children will not feel left out.

Dutch stereotypes have their in-built time slide: 'backwardness' may be overtaken by social climbing or, at least, by the adoption of symbolic markers of integration in dress and lifestyle. Yet the late Pim Fortuyn, the flamboyant Dutch politician whose party, the List Pim Fortuyn (LPF), shot up in the 2002 parliamentary elections, remained unequivocal in declaring Islam a 'backward' religion.

The test of how these boundaries are constructed, deconstructed and redrawn is in the neighbourhoods. Here residential familiarity makes it possible for distinctions to become fine, rather than crude generalizations, and to identify where they fade or are redefined. 'Our neighbour is a modern Turk', a statement made in an Amsterdam neighbourhood report, refers to the neighbour speaking Dutch (van Soest, 1994). Similar distinctions are drawn in neighbourhoods in Haarlem (de Jong, 1990). In districts of Amsterdam, Moroccan youths have taken over the haunts and street corners where previously Surinamese Creole boys gathered. The latter have moved on from the streets, first to youth centres and later to coffee shops and other commercial venues, a shift that was made earlier by white working-class youth (Sansone, 1992: 177). Accordingly, class patterns may turn out to be stronger than patterns based on cultural difference.

In France 'le droit à l'ambiguité' is claimed by the second and third generations of beurs, the audience of Rai and Rap music, and resisted by ethno-nationalists and Islamists (Gross et al., 1992). In the Netherlands, crossover is a common trend among second- and third-generation immigrants from Muslim countries (Feddema, 1992) and the resistance to cultural mixing is weak. What comes across in many reports is that what matters in the neighbourhoods is socio-economic prospects: jobs, education, living conditions, moving to a better area, and to some extent municipal and state policies, rather than cultural difference or 'ethnicity'. That these concerns are shared by immigrants and natives alike may be seen as a common reaction to living in the post-industrial welfare state.

However, rhetoric such as that articulated by Pim Fortuyn, referring to the country as 'full' and should therefore not accept any more immigrants, stirred up and rejuvenated many stereotypes in Dutch society. Previously, discussing immigrants and/or Islam in pejorative terms was considered taboo. This was no longer the case after Fortuyn arrived on the political scene, and ignited a racist discourse. Soon after his murder, the LPF gained 26 seats in the Parliamentary elections (previously they had none), which brought them level with the parties that had formed the previous coalition government. Subsequently, the party was invited to join the new coalition. The LPF managed to gain control over four ministries – including the Ministry of Immigration and Integration – a fact that left many immigrant groups uneasy and must have boosted the sense of injustice that Islamist thought thrives on. This is particularly noteworthy in light of the fact that after September 11, 2001, the Dutch newspaper *de Volkskrant* published an article in October 2001, with a photo of a plane in flames flying over New York City. The newspaper claims to have found this picture in a calendar hanging in a Muslim school. The implication of this and subsequent arrests of al-Qaʻeda suspects in the Netherlands in the summer of 2002, indicate that this European country has been used as a base for recruitment – although not for direct attacks.

Soon after the rise to power of the LPF, however, a number of its ministers were either ousted or arrested on allegations ranging from activity in a Surinamese militia to criminal records. Fighting and bickering within the LPF and their failure to get along with the other members of the coalition after extensive consultations (which the Dutch political system boasts of) resulted in the resignation of the government in October 2002. It is unlikely that Fortuyn's kind of rhetoric will resurface in new elections. But this episode does reveal a profound tension underlying multiculturalism: the rise in and consolidation of immigration coincided with cuts of the welfare state; precisely when greater investment in education, health care, housing and social services was needed, they were scaled down and the poor neighbourhoods suffered. In fact, it is not clear whether the issue is a crisis of multiculturalism or a crisis of the welfare state.

Whatever the outcome of this political drama however, the impact of political Islam in the Netherlands has not threatened contemporary discourse, although fertile grounds may lead it to flourish further, depending on the longevity of any anti-immigration rhetoric.

The flipside of the politics of post-Cold War Islam is that the negative media reporting of the defiance on the part of new forces rubs off on the Muslim diaspora. It contributes to a 'problem image' of Muslim minorities in the West, who are thereby kept on the periphery of the social imaginary, a dynamic that goes back for some time (e.g. Hargreaves et al., 1993).

The Jihad of al-Qa'eda seeks to convert Muslims travelling out (migration, quest for knowledge) into Muslims travelling in by turning emigrants into spiritual immigrants, warriors who put their skills and their lives to use in restoring the faith. Networks such as al-Qa'eda, while being part of Islamist globalism, underrate the pluralism of Islamic globalisms and ignore the many ways in which Islamic and western globalization are interwoven. In the process, they mirror western stereotypes of Islam, where the 'Islamic threat' is being exaggerated to serve geopolitical ends. Gilles Kepel (2002) argues that armed militancy in Bosnia, Algeria, Egypt and the September 11 attacks illustrate the weakness and failure of radical Islamism, rather than its accomplishment, because they are cut off from social movements on the ground. Such networks resemble Che Guevara's *focismo*, seeking to create a social movement through a spark of militancy.

Notes

1. Some parts of this this chapter first appeared in Jan Nederveen Pieterse, 'Travelling Islam: Mosques without Minarets', in Ayse Öncü and Petra Weyland (eds.). *Space, Culture and Power*, London: Zed Books, 1997, pp. 177–200.
2. Roughly a third of all Rotterdammers today are immigrants, and among the school-age population, the figure may be as high as two-thirds. Some are children of guestworkers from Turkey and Morocco. Unemployment is high in these communities.

References

Abdullah, Taufik. 'Islamic Society and the Challenge of Globalization', in J.A. Camilleri and C. Muzaffar (eds.). *Globalization: the Perspectives and Experiences of the Religious Traditions of Asia Pacific* (Petaling Jaya: International Movement for a Just World, 1998), pp. 51–62.

Aboutaleb, A. and van der Burght, F. 'De helden van de tweede generatie – jonge Turken en Marokkanen in Nederland', in S. Franke et al. (eds.). *Maak er een gewoonte van: racismebestrijding in de grote stad* (Amsterdam: De Populier, 1986) pp. 182–91.

Adas, Emin. 'The Prophet and Profit: the Rise of Islamist Entrepreneurs and New Interpretations of Islam in Turkey', University of Illinois at Urbana-Champaign, Transnational Studies Workshop Paper, 2002.

Adas, Michael (ed.). *Islamic and European Expansion: the Forging of a Global Order.* (Philadelphia: Temple University Press, 1993).

Ahmed, A.S and Donnan, H. (eds.). *Islam, Globalization and Postmodernity* (London: Routledge, 1994).

Ahmed, A.S. *Postmodernism and Islam* (London: Routledge, 1992).

Ali, Y. 'Muslim Women and the Politics of Ethnicity and Culture in North England', in G. Saghal and N. Yuval-Davis (eds.). *Refusing Holy Orders: Women and Fundamentalism in Britain* (London: Virago, 1992), pp. 101–23.

van Amersfoort, H. 'Ethnic Residential Patterns in a Welfare State: Lessons from Amsterdam 1970–1990', *New Community*, Vol. 18, No. 3, 1992, pp. 439–56.

Amin, S. 'Is There a Political Economy of Islamic Fundamentalism?' in *Delinking* (London: Zed Books, 1990), pp. 174–88.

Antoun, Richard T. 'Sojourners Abroad: Migration for Higher Education in a Post-Peasant Society', in Akbar S. Ahmed and H. Donnan (eds.). *Islam, Globalization and Postmodernity* (London: Routledge, 1994), pp. 160–89.

Armstrong, Karen. 'Islam through History', in J.F. Hoge Jr and G. Rose (eds.). *How Did This Happen? Terrorism and the New War*, (New York, Public Affairs, 2001), pp. 53–70.

Atasoy, Seymen. 'Globalization and Turkey: From Capitulations to Contemporary Civilization', in S.T. Ismael (ed.). *Globalization: Policies, Challenges and Responses* (Calgary, Alberta: Detselig, 1999), pp. 257–70.

Al-Azmeh, A. *Islams and Modernities* (London: Verso, 1993).

Bartels, E. 'Moslimvrouwen en moslim-identiteit', in R. Haleber (ed.). *Rushdie effecten: afwijzing van moslim-identiteit in Nederland?* (Amsterdam: SUA, 1989) pp. 171–7.

Beeley, B. 'Islam as a Global Political Force', in A.G. McGrew, P.G. Lewis et al. *Global Politics* (Cambridge: Polity, 1992), pp. 293–311.

van den Berg-Eldering, L. 'Moslims als minderheid in Nederland', in *De Arabische wereld en haar minderheden* (Katwijk: Nederlands-Arabische Kring, 1985), pp. 69–78.

Beunders, H. and Huygen, M. 'Een zuil zonder fundament', *NRC Handelsblad*, 22 April 1989.

Bird, J. et al. (eds.). *Mapping the Futures: Local Cultures, Global Change* (London: Routledge, 1993).

Boomtown Amsterdam: ontwerpen om de stad (Amsterdam: ARCAM/ Meulenhoff, 1988).

Brugman, J. *De zuilen van de Islam* (Amsterdam: Meulenhoff, 1985).

Camilleri, J.A. and Muzaffar, C. (eds.). *Globalization: the Perspectives and Experiences of the Religious Traditions of Asia Pacific* (Petaling Jaya: International Movement for a Just World, 1998).

Christie, C.J. 'The Rope of God: Muslim Minorities in the West and Britain', *New Community*, Vol. 17, No. 3, 1991, pp. 457–66.

Cross, M. (ed.). *Ethnic Minorities and Industrial Change in Europe and North America* Cambridge (Cambridge: Cambridge University Press, 1992).

Darsh, S.M. *Muslims in Europe* (London: Ta-Ha, 1980).

Eickelmann, D.F. and Piscatori, J. (eds.). *Muslim travelers: Pilgrimage, Migration, and the Religious Imagination* (Berkeley: University of California Press, 1990).

Feddema, R. 'Levensoriëntatie van jonge Turken en Marokkanen in Nederland', PhD dissertation, Utrecht University, 1992.

Franke, S. et al. (eds.). *Maak er een gewoonte van: racismebestrijding in de grote stad* (Amsterdam: De Populier, 1992).

Fuller, G.E. and Lesser, I.O. *A Sense of Siege: the Geopolitics of Islam and the West* (Boulder, Colorado: Westview Press, 1995).

Geertz, C. *Islam Observed: Religious Development in Morocco and Indonesia* (Chicago: Chicago University Press, 1968).

George, D. 'Pax Islamica: an Alternative New World Order', unpublished paper, University of Newcastle, 1993.

Gerholm, T. and Lithman, Y.G. (eds.). *The New Islamic Presence in Western Europe* (London: Mansell, 1988).

Gilsenan, M. *Recognizing Islam* (New York: Pantheon, 1982).

Gross, J., McMurray, D. and Swedenborg, T. 'Rai, Rap and Ramadan Nights: Franco-Maghribi Cultural Identities', *Middle East Report*, Vol. 22, No. 5, 1992, pp. 11–16.

Haleber, R. (ed.). *Rushdie effecten: afwijzing van moslim-identiteit in Nederland?* (Amsterdam: SUA, 1989).

Halliday, F. *Islam and the Myth of Confrontation* (London: I.B. Tauris, 1995).

Hamel, P., Lustiger-Thaler, H., Nederveen Pieterse, J. and Roseneil, S. (eds.). *Globalization and Social Movements* (Basingstoke and New York: Palgrave, 2001).

Hargreaves, A.G. and Perotti, A. 'The Representation of French Television of Immigrants and Ethnic Minorities of Third World Origin', *New Community*, Vol. 19, No. 2, 1993, pp. 251–62.

Hoge, J.F. Jr. and Rose, G. (eds.). *How Did This Happen? Terrorism and the New War* (New York: Public Affairs, 2001).

de Jong, A.T. *Interetnische verhoudingen in een overbelaste nieuwbouwwijk* (Rijswijk: Ministerie van WVC, Onderzoek en Perspectief), No. 12, 1990.

Karagül, A. and Wagtendonk, K. *De imâms* (Den Haag: Islamitische Raad Nederland, 1994).

Kepel, Gilles. *Jihad: the Trail of Political Islam* (Cambridge, MA: Belknap Press and Harvard University Press, 2002).

Knippenberg, H. and de Pater, B. *De eenwording van Nederland* (Nijmegen: SUN, 1988).

Kolbert, Elizabeth. 'Beyond Tolerance: What did the Dutch See in Pim Fortyn?', *The New Yorker*, 9 September 2002, pp. 106–14.

Kuran, T. 'The Economic Impact of Islamic Fundamentalism', in Martin Marty and R. Scott Appleby (eds.). *Fundametalisms and the State*, The Fundamentalism Project, Vol. 3 (Chicago: University of Chicago Press, 1993).

Landman, N. *Van mat tot minaret* (Amsterdam: Vrije Universiteit Press, 1992).

Lewis, B. *What Went Wrong? Western Impact and Middle Eastern Response* (New York: Oxford University Press, 2001).

Mardin, S. 'The Nakshibendi Order of Turkey', in Martin Marty and R. Scott Appleby (eds.). *Fundamentalisms and the State*, The Fundamentalism Project, Vol. 3 (Chicago, University of Chicago Press, 1983), pp. 204–32.

Marty, Martin and Scott Appleby, R. (eds.). *Fundamentalisms and the State*, The Fundamentalism Project, Vol. 3 (Chicago: University of Chicago Press, 1993).

Massey, D. 'Power-geometry and a Progressive Sense of Place', in J. Bird et al. (eds.). *Mapping the Futures: Local Cultures, Global Change* (London: Routledge, 1993), pp. 59–69.

Miles, R. and Satzewich, V. 'Migration, Racism and "Postmodern" Capitalism', *Economy and Society*, Vol. 19, No. 3, 1990, pp. 334–58.

Modood, T. 'Muslim Views on Religious Identity and Racial Equality', *New Community*, Vol. 19, No. 3, 1993, pp. 513–20.

Nederveen Pieterse, J.P. 'Transnational Alliances and the Dutch Revolution: the Politics of the Transition from Feudalism to Capitalism', unpublished paper, 1983.

——. '"Fundamentalism" Discourses: Enemy Images', in *Women against Fundamentalism*, Vol. 1, No. 5, 1994, pp. 2–6.

——. 'Hybrid Modernities: Mélange Modernities in Asia', *Sociological Analysis*, Vol. 1, No. 3, 1998, pp. 75–86.

——. 'Collective Action and Globalization', in P. Hamel, H. Lustiger-Thaler, J. Nederveen Pieterse and S. Roseneil (eds.). *Globalization and Social Movements* (London and New York: Palgrave, 2001), pp. 21–40.

Nielsen, J.S. *Muslims in Western Europe* (Edinburgh: Edinburgh University Press, 1992).

Obbema, J. 'Winkelen met een tas vol heimwee', *NRC Handelsblad*, 10 March 1994.

Parekh, B. 'Between Holy Text and Moral Void', in A. Gray and J. McGuigan (eds.). *Studying Culture* (London: Edward Arnold, 1993), pp. 139–46.

Pellerin, H. 'Global Restructuring and the Transnationalisation of Migration Limits and Promises of the Movement of People in the Emerging World Order', unpublished paper, 1994.

Pijper, G.F. *Islam and the Netherlands* (Leiden: E.J. Brill, 1957).

Pred, A. and Watts, M.J. *Reworking Modernity: Capitalisms and Symbolic Discontent* (New Brunswick, NJ: Rutgers University Press, 1992).

Rath, J., Groenendijk, K. and Penninx, R. 'The Recognition and Institutionalisation of Islam in Belgium, Great Britain and the Netherlands', *New Community*, Vol. 18, No. 1, 1991, pp. 101–14.

Reedijk, W. 'Rushdie, Racisme en Antiracisme in Een Buurt', in R. Haleber (ed.). *Rushdie effecten: afwijzing van moslim-identiteit in Nederland?* (Amsterdam: SUA, 1989), pp. 158–68.

Saghal, G. and Yuval-Davis, N. (eds.). *Refusing Holy Orders: Women and Fundamentalism in Britain* (London: Virago, 1992).

Sansone, L. *Schitteren in de Schaduw: Overlevingsstrategieën, Subcultuur en Etniciteit van Creoolse Jongeren Uit de Lagere Klasse in Amsterdam 1981–1990* (Amsterdam: Spinhuis, 1992).

Sassen, S. *The Global City: New York, London, Tokyo* (Princeton, NJ: Princeton University Press, 1991).

Sassen, S. 'Rethinking Immigration', *Lusitania*, Vol. 5, 1993, pp. 97–102.

Schiffauer, W. 'Migration and Religiousness', in T. Gerholm and Y.G. Lithman (eds.). *The New Islamic Presence in Western Europe* (London: Mansell, 1988), pp. 146–58.

Sen, F. 'Islamischer Fundamentalismus und die türkische Minderheit in der Bundesrepublik Deutschland', in T. Meyer (ed.). *Fundamentalismus in der modernen Welt* (Frankfurt: Suhrkamp, 1989), pp. 296–303.

Shadid, W.A.R. and van Koningsveld, P.S. (eds.) *Islam in Dutch Society* (Kampen: Kok Pharos, 1992).

Sijtsma, J. 'De Rushdie affaire in de Marokkaanse moskeeën in Nederland', in R. Haleber (ed.). *Rushdie effecten: afwijzing van moslim-identiteit in Nederland?* (Amsterdam: SUA, 1989), pp. 149–57.

Slomp, J. 'Moskeeën in Nederland', *Prana* Vol. 38, 1984, pp. 47–53.

——. 'Moslim minderheden in Nederland', in *Islamitische stromingen in Nederland* (Amsterdam: Vrije Universiteit, 1985), pp. 7–20.

al-Turabi, H. 'Islam as a Pan-National Movement and Nation-States: an Islamic Doctrine on Human Association', unpublished paper, 1993.

Veraart, J. 'Turkish Coffeehouses in Holland', *Migration*, Vol. 3, 1993, pp. 97–114.

de Vries, M. *Ogen in je rug: Turkse meisjes en jonge vrouwen in Nederland* (Alphen aan de Rijn: Samsom, 1987).

Waardenburg, J. 'The Institutionalization of Islam in the Netherlands 1961–86', in T. Gerholm and Y.G. Lithman (eds.). *The New Islamic Presence in Western Europe* (London: Mansell, 1988), pp. 8–31.

Zakaria, Rafiq. *The Struggle within Islam: the Conflict between Religion and Politics* (London: Penguin, 1989).

5
Cognac, Cigarettes and Terrorist Cells in Albania

Frederick C. Abrahams

In the summer of 1992, months after the fall of Albania's repressive communist regime, a group of eager Evangelists from the United States travelled to a remote village in Albania to spread the good word. Like hundreds of missionaries – Moonies, Hari Krishna and Scientologists – they had come after communism's collapse to save the Albanian soul. The Americans promised to build a church and then found a local man who was willing, for a fee, to be minister. After some training and a delivery of Bibles, they left him to his work. The next summer, the Americans returned to check on the church and its minister. To their dismay, the church had been converted into a mosque and the man they had appointed as minister was the local imam. 'What happened?' the Americans asked. 'Even God needs to be paid,' the man said, explaining that Islamic visitors had offered him a better deal.

Albanians, most of whom are Muslim, can't agree whether this story is a fact or a joke. Regardless, it sheds light on Albanians' unique relationship to religion. First, after 45 years under Europe's most isolated and orthodox communist regime, the continent's poorest country is open to religious influences from around the world. Second, and more significantly, religion does not play a major role in the Albanian identity. Throughout history, Albanians have often chosen religion for pragmatic and even opportunistic reasons, rather than religious zeal.

These facts help explain why, ten years after communism's fall, Europe's only Muslim-majority country has mostly kept Islamic states and movements at a distance. While radical Islamic groups have taken advantage of Albania's poverty and post-communist chaos, leading to CIA arrests, closed embassies and heated political debates, political Islam has not had a major impact on the country's people or government. As this chapter will show, Albania's relationship with Islam is complex and at times contradictory, but political Islam has not taken root.

Roughly the size of Maryland, in the United States, Albania has a population of approximately 3.3 million. An estimated 70 per cent of the people are Muslim, 20 per cent Christian Orthodox and 10 per cent Catholic. As in Bosnia, the Islamic community converted from Christianity during the 500 years of Ottoman rule because of pressure and tax incentives provided by the Turks. Continuing a tradition of loyal service to the ruling empire, many Albanians then served in the Ottoman civil service, including top-ranking political and military officers.

Albanian Muslims, most of them Sunni, have never been fervent believers in the faith. Especially in the South, the predominant sect is Bekteshi, which originated in Anatolia around the thirteenth century, and is known for its tolerant and pantheistic beliefs. In Albania, members of the sect are jokingly referred to as 'sex, drug and rock and roll Muslims' because of their liberal views. As an Albanian journalist writing about Islam in the country observed, most Albanian Muslims start their day with cognac, cigarettes and a coffee.[1]

Despite occasional friction, the three major faiths have tradition-ally coexisted. The three religions worked together during the Albanian National Awakening of the nineteenth century at the end of the Ottoman Empire, showing how Albanian ethnic identity is stronger than religious ties. This is expressed in the oft-quoted line of the Albanian poet Pashko Vasa, who wrote 'the religion of the Albanian is Albanianism'.

Some historians believe that cooperation among the religions helped Albania gain independence in 1912.[2] Others have suggested that the lack of a dominant religion, as there is in Serbia, Croatia and Greece, has weakened the Albanian national movement and made the country susceptible to invasion.[3] Albania gained its indepen-dence later than other countries in the region and has remained Europe's poorest state. Since 1912, it has been occupied by seven different armies (Italy twice).

Albania's harsh communism, run for 45 years by the dictator Enver Hoxha, further muted religion's call. Hundreds of priests and muftis were imprisoned or executed. Catholics in the north were viewed as Vatican spies. In 1967 Hoxha declared Albania the world's first officially atheist state. The country's mosques and churches were turned into community centres and sports halls. The cathedral in the northern town of Shkoder was turned into a basketball court with 'Praise Marxism-Leninism' inscribed in red above the hoops.

In 1990, as communism was falling, the Catholics in Shkoder were the first to challenge the regime by holding a public mass. Later, the community encouraged Shkoder's Muslim cleric to open the mosque in defiance of the state, because it would be better for religious freedom to 'fly with two wings', as an employee at Shkoder's church explained.[4] The cleric hesitated out of fear of the still powerful secret police, so the Catholics threatened to dynamite his house if he did not comply. It was an ironic and powerful example of religious tolerance and pragmatism in Albania: open your mosque or we'll blow up your house!

Religious coexistence has mostly continued since communism's collapse two and a half years after the fall of the Berlin Wall. As an unspoken power-sharing agreement, it is customary for the president, prime minister and speaker of parliament to be divided among the faiths. Denied religious ceremonies for so long, some Albanians celebrate both Christmas and Bajram (the Muslim holy feast). Just after communism's fall, young Muslims wore crucifixes as a pro-western act of defiance.

Culturally, Albanians are divided between East and West. Like an American crossing the street in London, they do not know which way to look. Music has an Eastern flair but cultural icons come from Hollywood and Italian TV. Albanians drink sweet Turkish coffee, but their most famous personality is Mother Teresa. The national hero Skenderbeg, who was born Catholic, converted to Islam and then returned to the Catholic Church and fought to defend Christian Europe from Ottoman encroachment.

Pragmatism Rules

On 21 June 1991, James Baker, the famously unflappable US Secretary of State, had what he described as the proudest moment of his diplomatic career. On a sweltering day, he arrived at Rinas Airport in Tirana, the capital of Albania, for a seven-hour visit to show US support for ongoing reform. A communist president was still in power.

Delirious crowds mobbed the convoy from the airport, hoping to glimpse or touch the guest from the West. Eager men threw flowers on the delegation's cars, kissed the windscreens and tried to carry Baker's limousine into Tirana. The delegation drove to the city's

Skenderbeg Square, where more than 300,000 Albanians waved small American flags mass-produced by the country's first non-communist opposition group, the Democratic Party. 'I have come here today to bring you a message from another free people,' Baker told the jubilant crowd. 'Welcome to the assembly of free people building a Europe whole and free. You are with us, and we are with you,' he declared.[5]

Baker's reception signified Albanians' great desire to turn towards the West. After 50 years of orthodox Stalinism which forbade religion, banned private property and executed dissenters – independent of the 'imperialist West' and the 'revisionist East' – the impoverished population was eager to 'rejoin Europe'. The first non-communist government, elected in March 1992, pursued the 'go West' path. Albania became the first East European country to request membership of NATO and aligned itself politically and economically with Europe and the United States. The Democratic Party sought membership in Europe's Christian Democratic Union.

It therefore came as a surprise to most Albanians when the country's first democratically elected president, Sali Berisha, began to court the Islamic world. Throughout late 1992, Berisha expanded relations with Muslim states in North Africa and the Gulf, which promised aid and offered to build and renovate mosques destroyed during communism. Albanian government delegations visited Egypt, Libya, Kuwait and Iran to seek financial assistance, as well as support for the Muslims in Bosnia and the ethnic Albanians in Kosovo.[6]

The most dramatic moment for the Albanian public came in December 1992, when Berisha travelled to Saudi Arabia and, without previous public discussion, announced that Albania had gained full membership in the Organization of Islamic Conference (OIC). Under the communist government, Albania had gained observer status in the Conference one year earlier, but that was viewed as a move to parry the West, which was pressing for democratic reform. At the time, Albania was surviving on humanitarian aid from Catholic Italy and remittances from Albanians working in Orthodox Greece.

Most Albanians were shocked, including some members of government who had not been apprised of the decision. Parliament refused to ratify the agreement. Some of the country's leading intellectuals threatened to convert to Christianity in protest. The country's future was with Italy, France, Germany, England and the United States, they said. Berisha's choice reflected more than the divided East–West identity that Albanians confront; it was the result of pragmatic politics after the Cold War. Like the opportunistic conversion to Islam 600 years before, or the poor villager choosing the mosque over the church, tactical decisions determined Islam's role.

Berisha defended his move on economic grounds. The foreign aid coming from the West was not satisfactory, he said, and the Islamic countries had promised huge amounts of support. The condition for economic support, Berisha informed the government, was that Albania joins the OIC. He hoped this would provide desperately needed aid and push the West to open its coffers. 'There is no tendency to see religion play a political role in Albania,' President Berisha said, trying to counter allegations that Albania was becoming an Islamic republic.[7] To stress the point, he invited Pope John Paul II and NATO Secretary General Manfred Werner to Albania.

The Arab Albanian Islamic Bank soon opened in Tirana – the first foreign bank to set up in the country – but the money never flowed in. According to Genc Ruli, the Albanian Finance Minister at the time, money from Islamic states mostly went to rebuilding mosques or Islamic education. In late 1992, he said, the Islamic Development Bank gave US$1 million to the Ministry of Education for the publication of copies of the Qur'an.[8]

Berisha had other reasons for joining the OIC, former and present Albanian government officials now admit. In addition to economic aid, he was garnering support for the Bosnian Muslims, at war with Bosnian Serbs, and the ethnic Albanians in Kosovo, also Muslim, who were facing repression by the Serbian state. Indeed, over the coming years, the OIC passed a number of resolutions condemning Serbian state violence in Kosovo. More concretely, Berisha offered Albania as a gateway to Bosnia for arms and foreign fighters, despite a UN arms embargo on Yugoslavia. He did this with the knowledge of the West, which was striving to establish a balance of power in the region. It was also a message to the Serbs that, should fighting spread to Kosovo, the ethnic Albanians there could expect help.

The December 1992 Organization of Islamic Conference meeting in Jeddah, during which Albania became a full member, was convened specifically to discuss the war in Bosnia-Herzegovina. Bosnian President Alija Izetbegovic was in attendance, as were the West's chief negotiators, Cyrus Vance and Lord Owen. According to a cable from the US consul in Jeddah, obtained through a Freedom of Information Act request, there was a comment on almost every conference participant's lips: 'Bosnia must be allowed to receive arms to help in its defence.'[9] The prime minister of the Kosovo Albanian shadow government, Bujar Bukoshi, was also in Jeddah at the time, and he had participated in previous OIC meetings.[10]

Saudi Arabia's King Fahd opened the meeting, flanked by Izetbegovic and Berisha, saying that Bosnia should have the opportunity to obtain the weapons it needs for self-defence.[11] Izetbegovic followed with an impassioned ten-minute speech, in which he asked whether the world's 'indifference' was because the victims in Bosnia were Muslim or because the world did not care. Referring to the arms embargo on the former Yugoslavia, he accused those who 'bind our hands' of being accomplices in Bosnia's tragedy, and then asked for 'limited quantities' of defensive weapons.[12]

Albanian President Berisha followed with what the US embassy cable on the meeting called a 'somewhat rambling diatribe'. The Albanian leader attacked the anti-Muslim policies of Slobodan Milosevic and what he called 'Serbian Orthodox fundamentalists'. With public pressure in the member states building, a conference resolution reaffirmed Bosnia's right to individual and collective self-defence, in accordance with the UN Charter, and called on the Security Council to lift the arms embargo on Bosnia.

Behind the scenes, Albania became a transit point for arms to Bosnia, according to former and present Albanian officials.[13] Arms purchased from Muslim states, most probably Saudi Arabia, Libya and Iran, were transported through Albania to the Bosnian Muslim army. Some *mujaheddin* also made their way through Albania en route to Bosnia during this time. An estimated 3,000 *mujaheddin* fought at some stage in Bosnia in at least three special units for foreign fighters, including one called El-Mudzahid under the command of the Bosnian Army's Third Corps.[14]

This arrangement continued until the Dayton Agreement in December 1995 ended the fighting in Bosnia. The El-Mudzahid unit was disbanded, reportedly on orders from the US, which wanted to break Bosnia's Islamic ties, but an estimated 300 Islamic fighters stayed in Bosnia, some of them getting citizenship.[15] Post-September 11 sweeps ordered by the US have arrested some of those who stayed behind, leading to legally questionable extraditions, but others remain integrated peacefully into Bosnian society.[16] An undetermined number of *mujaheddin* came to Albania after the war, hoping to make it a European base.

Fight for Souls

Islamic organizations had been coming to Albania since James Baker's visit in 1991, when Albania was opening to the world. After

50 years of enforced atheism, religious groups of all sorts prosely-tized throughout the country. White-shirted Mormons roamed the dusty streets and L. Ron Hubbard's *Dianetics* was available in bookshops. Especially after Albania joined the Islamic Conference, various charities from Islamic states established operations to assist orphans, provide humanitarian aid or construct mosques, which began appearing in villages around Albania, sometimes with visual instructions outside on how to pray. Businesses from Kuwait and Saudi Arabia began working in fields like construction.

While there is no evidence that these legitimate charities or businesses were involved in terrorist activities, and many of them contributed to Albania's development, Albanian officials admit that some of them unknowingly provided cover for individuals with less pure intentions. According to a member of the Albanian intelligence service, known as the SHIK, who works on anti-terrorist activity, the French, British and American governments started warning the Albanian government in 1993 about the presence in Albania of indi-viduals connected to various 'terrorist organizations', specifically the Algerian Armed Islamic Group (GIA) and the al-Jihad (Egyptian Islamic Jihad), who were using charities as cover.[17]

GIA has fought to overthrow the Algerian government since early 1992, just after the Algerian government declared the 1991 electoral victory of the Islamic Salvation Front (FIS) – the largest Islamic party – void. Egyptian Jihad, run by Ayman al-Zawahri, has claimed responsibility for attacks on top Egyptian government officials, including the 1981 assassination of President Anwar Sadat.

For individuals in these organizations, Albania was the perfect place. The dismantling of extreme communism created a Wild East environment, where illegal activities thrived in the maze of porous borders, fragile laws and corruption. With a weak police and judiciary, and its proximity to Italy, Albania became the ideal location for small cells to establish a base. According to past and present members of the Albanian SHIK, the Albanian government and numerous articles in the Albanian and international press, Egyptian Jihad set up small cells for logistics, with their members integrating quietly into the community.[18] With its lawlessness, Albania became a centre for money laundering, as well as for organizing transit to the West.

The then Albanian government's role in supporting these groups remains unclear. Although there is no evidence to suggest the government knowingly assisted such organizations, corrupt government officials provided residence permits and sometimes passports to the Islamic charities and businesses, perhaps unaware that some employees were involved in more nefarious activities. More questionable is the role of Berisha's SHIK, run at the time by Bashkim Gazidede, who was also head of Albania's Organization of Islamic Intellectuals. On the one hand, SHIK cooperated with the CIA by monitoring Islamic organizations in the country, with equipment and training provided by the Americans.[19] Berisha gladly used the equipment to keep track of his political opposition.

On the other hand, particularly after September 11, allegations have emerged about Gazidede's relations with Islamic organizations, including a supposed visit of bin Laden to Albania in 1994.[20] After the fall of the Berisha government in 1997, Gazidede fled to Turkey and then reportedly to either Iran, Syria or Libya.[21] Albanian media reports claim that, in winter 2002, he sought asylum in the United States, but this remains unconfirmed.

Thus far, no concrete evidence linking Gazidede or Berisha to radical Islamist organizations has emerged, aside from their *laissez-faire* policy towards questionable foreign organizations. Some of the criticism can be discounted as attempts by Albania's neighbours – Serbia, Macedonia and Greece – to discredit the country, as well as the current Albanian government's desire to undermine Berisha, who fell from power after the collapse of shady 'pyramid schemes' in 1997.

Berisha supporters counter that illegal organizations proliferated in the anarchy of the pyramid scheme's collapse, after Berisha had been ousted. In an interview in the Albanian press, former SHIK official Bujar Rama admitted the presence of some 'terrorists' during the Berisha government, but claimed they were monitored in cooperation with 'counterpart services'. 'The vacuum created by the lack of law and order in Albania [in 1997],' he said, 'created the opportunity for the formation of organizations, armed gangs and for organized crime to establish a strong basis and have connections with criminal organizations in the world.'[22]

Clampdown

The Albanian government that followed Berisha, run by the former Communist Party, worked hard to re-establish good relations with the US government and the CIA, which had deteriorated toward the end of Berisha's rule. It also downgraded Albania's relations with the

Islamic world. After assuming power, the new prime minister, Fatos Nano, declared that Albania's participation in the Organization of Islamic Conference was 'not on my government's agenda'.[23] Foreign Minister Pascal Milo declared Albania's OIC membership 'a constitutional violation' because it had never been ratified by parliament.[24]

The new government understood that, by late 1997, the regional and international political scene had dramatically changed. First, after eight years of passive resistance to Serbian government repression, an armed independence movement began to form among ethnic Albanians in the neighbouring region of Kosovo, known as the Kosovo Liberation Army (KLA). At the same time, international terrorism had become an issue in Washington, and the Albanian government was open to cooperation.

The KLA was aware of the new mood and, eager for western support, worked hard to distance itself from any association with Islamic groups. According to former members of the KLA, the Albanian SHIK and press reports, the rebels refused assistance from Muslim countries, including offers of arms and fighters, on orders from the US government.[25] Some KLA leaders were inherently adverse to assistance from religious groups because of their Marxist-Leninist political leanings. Throughout the Kosovo war in 1998 and 1999, the KLA had more volunteers from western countries such as Germany and Holland than from any Islamic state.

In June 1998, Albanian police arrested Claude Kader, a French citizen believed to be of Middle East origin, after he shot and killed his Albanian interpreter in Tirana. At his trial, Kader told an Albanian court that he had been sent to Albania by bin Laden to assist the KLA, but the Kosovars had rejected his help.[26] The KLA's lack of central control allowed a few *mujaheddin* to slip through. According to Serbian and Albanian sources, on 18 July 1998, 24 Islamic volunteers set out for Kosovo through the mountains of northern Albania with a group of approximately 200 KLA fighters. Six kilometres into Kosovo, near the Djeravica and Kosara border posts, Yugoslav forces ambushed the group, killing 18 of the foreign fighters and four Albanians.[27] According to a KLA member who was present, one 82 mm shell killed four of the *mujaheddin*.[28] It is not clear whether the group was caught due to Yugoslav vigilance or a leak by those eager to keep Islamic fighters out of the region.

Around the same time, the CIA began to crack down on the Egyptian al-Jihad cells operating in Albania. The Egyptian group had recently merged with al-Qa'eda to form the International Islamic

Front for Jihad against Jews and Crusaders, with the goal of targeting US and Israeli interests. The head of Egyptian Jihad, Ayman al-Zawahri, reportedly became bin Laden's right-hand man.

In June and July 1998, SHIK forces, in cooperation with the CIA, arrested five members of Egyptian Jihad who had been active in Albania, including two men previously sentenced to death *in absentia* by an Egyptian court for terrorist acts.[29] Albanian agents killed one man in his apartment after he opened fire from a washing machine where he was hiding, according to a SHIK agent with knowledge of the action.[30] After interrogation by the CIA at a remote airbase, the men were extradited without a judge's order on a US government plane to Egypt.

Just after the arrests, the Islamic Observation Centre in London sent an open letter to Albanian President Rexhep Mejdani warning against the detainees' extradition to Egypt. 'We warn that these suspect practices that contradict the most basic tenets of human rights and the teaching of our true religion will lead only to defeats and the wrath of Allah and Muslims,' the letter said.[31] On 5 August, a letter appeared in an Arab newspaper in London signed by the International Islamic Front for Jihad Against Jews and Crusaders, which vowed revenge for the arrests in Albania in a 'language they will understand'.[32]

Two days later, bombs exploded outside the US embassies in Kenya and Tanzania, killing 224 people. It is not clear whether the attacks had been planned in advance or whether they were in direct retaliation for the Albanian operation. Given the extent of planning and preparation reportedly involved in terrorist acts, it is likely that the timing was coincidental.

The US government took no chances. On 14 August, the US embassy in Tirana, a villa in central Tirana, suspended normal activities and sent home non-essential staff. Two hundred Marines and ten Navy SEALS were deployed to protect the housing compound on the outskirts of Tirana that served as a temporary embassy until the proper embassy could be reinforced.[33] The State Department urged Americans not to travel in Albania and US officials spoke of a 'credible threat from an Islamic terrorist organization'.[34]

That winter, the trial of the extradited Egyptians began in the Haikstep military camp outside Cairo, along with 107 other defendants, 64 of them *in absentia*.[35] The trial, dubbed the 'trial of the Albanian returnees', was Egypt's largest terrorism case since Egyptian Jihad members had been tried for the assassination of

Sadat. In total, 87 people were convicted, ten of whom were executed, including two of the men arrested in Albania.[36]

According to confessions and investigative reports provided to journalists by the defence, the five people extradited from Albania all complained of torture in Albania and Egypt.[37] The detainees spoke of beatings, electric shocks to the genitals and standing for hours in cold water. Although the allegations of torture cast doubt on the credibility of the confessions, the testimonies, when pieced together, shed light on the Egyptian Jihad operations in Albania.

According to the documents, Ayman al-Zawahri's younger brother, Mohammed, was the first to arrive in Albania and began working for the Islamic Relief Organization, one of many Islamic charities based in the country. He began placing jobs for other Egyptian al-Jihad members in charities, recruiting a forger, propagandist and dues collector. Egyptian Jihad provided logistical support for the al-Qa'eda network, transferring money, forging travel documents and facilitating communications.

September 11, 2001

Since the extradition, the Albanian government and the Berisha-led opposition have both maintained a pro-American stance, especially after the September 11 attacks. Both sides accuse the other of being insufficiently red, white and blue.[38] The Albanian government expressed its full solidarity with the Western camp and offered Albanian troops to fight in Afghanistan.[39] Albanian authorities have strengthened anti-terrorist legislation, tightened border controls and screened foreigners in the country.

On 13 September, Tirana's police chief claimed that Albania was no longer a safe haven for Islamic political organizations. The police had expelled 'at least a dozen Islamic activists – notably Egyptians, Saudis and Iraqis – suspected of being responsible for a number of criminal acts,' he said.[40] The next day, an official day of mourning in Albania for the September 11 victims, US ambassador to Albania, Joseph Limprecht, announced that there was no terrorist threat in the country. The accuracy of the claim is hard to determine given Albania's porous borders, fragile legal state and endemic corruption. But without question, 'wanted' political groups found it more difficult to operate.

Continuing its anti-terrorist drive, in January 2002 Albanian authorities froze the assets of a Saudi businessman, Yasin al-Qadi, accused by the US of laundering money for the al-Qa'eda network. The government sequestered two 17-storey buildings under construction by al-Qadi's company in central Tirana, ironically known as 'the twin towers'. Al-Qadi, who runs the Saudi-based Muwafaq Foundation, said the decision to freeze his assets was 'politically motivated' and 'runs contrary to international law'.[41]

Not to be outdone by Albanians in Albania, Kosovar Albanians expressed their sincere solidarity with the victims in the US, holding silent vigils and writing letters of condolence to the US government. Displaying Albanians' relaxed attitude towards religion, a Muslim man at a community meeting in Gjakova even proposed destroying the town's mosques as a sign of pro-western intent. The suggestion was refused.

Grateful for NATO's intervention against Yugoslavia, the KLA went to great lengths to distance itself from any Islamic connection. The successor to the KLA, an ostensibly civil organization known as the Kosovo Protection Corps, lined up to donate blood for the victims. A joke in Kosovo says that, after the donation, looting in New York soared.

The Region

Despite these efforts, Albania's neighbours, notably the Serbian and Macedonian governments, have taken advantage of September 11 to present Albania and Albanians as an Islamic threat to Europe. In his war crimes trial in The Hague, former Yugoslav President Slobodan Milosevic claimed that the KLA had ties to bin Laden and the 'al-Qaeda branch in Kosovo'.[42] In Macedonia, where an armed ethnic Albanian group called the National Liberation Army (NLA) has been fighting for improved rights within the country, the government has tried to link the Albanian rebels to *mujaheddin* and what it calls Islamic terrorist forces.

On 2 March 2002, Macedonian police shot and killed seven men they identified as *mujaheddin* who, the government claimed, were planning attacks on government officials and foreign embassies. NLA uniforms were found in the terrorists' bags, the government said. Some diplomats in the country doubted the story, viewing it as a government attempt to win western support for the struggle against the NLA.[43] Although the evidence is not yet conclusive, the NLA or other armed ethnic Albanian groups may have some Islamic elements, just as the KLA allowed some *mujaheddin* to slip through. But these elements appear marginal and can be attributed to the dispersed and disorganized nature of rebel movements in the region. Although religion plays more of a role among Albanians outside Albania, especially in Macedonia, the allegiance is still strongly with the West.

In Albania, despite the comings and goings of various political Islamic groups over the years, Islamist movements have had little impact on the country, other than as another issue over which the government and opposition can squabble. The competition is over how demonstrably both sides can stay away. The danger is perhaps in the government's overzealous attempts to eradicate any outside Islamic presence, at the cost of civil liberties. Arabs living in Albania have been interrogated and legitimate Islamic charities might be closed. An analogy can be drawn with the first years of Albania's transition, when the West, and particularly the US, strongly supported the Berisha government because of its cooperative approach to Kosovo, Macedonia and the war in the former Yugoslavia, despite authoritarianism at home. Today, Washington may tolerate human rights abuses by the Socialist-led government in Albania because of its contributions to the new international crisis: the 'war on terror'.

As it did with Berisha, the western approach may fail unless accompanied by genuine efforts to build democratic institutions, the rule of law and a stable economy in Albania. Radical foreign groups can be more easily blocked when trafficking, smuggling and money laundering are not pervasive aspects of Albanian life. In the meantime, Albanian society is largely pro-West. Poverty may cause some people to choose the mosque over the church, or the church over the mosque, depending on the offer. But, as has been the case throughout Albania's difficult history, these will often be choices of the stomach more than the mind.

Notes

1. Bejtja (1999).
2. Skeni (1967).
3. Fischer (1999: 52).
4. Interview with author, Shkoder, Albania, 20 February 2001.
5. Curtius (1991). See also Baker and DeFrank (1995: 485).
6. Cable from US Embassy, Tirana, Albania, to Secretary of State, Washington, DC, 01978, 121435Z, November 1992. Albanian government trips to these countries are well documented in the Albanian press.

7. Agence France Presse, 27 November 1992.
8. Interview with author, Tirana, Albania, 11 February 2002.
9. Cable from US Consul, Jeddah, Saudi Arabia to Secretary of State, Washington, DC, 02301, 011534Z, December 1992.
10. 'Bukoshi Asks Aid of Islamic States', *Illyria*, 2 December 1992. See also Radin (1992).
11. Murphy (1992). See also Ford (1992).
12. US cable, 011534Z.
13. Interviews with author.
14. The existence of the El-Mudzahid unit is well documented by international organizations, the Bosnian and international press and testimony from the International Criminal Tribunal for the Former Yugoslavia (ICTY). See, for example, 'Bin Laden and the Balkans: the Politics of Anti-Terrorism', International Crisis Group, 9 November 2001, p. 11; 'Islamic Groups from BiH Are on the American List', *Slobodna Dalmacija*, 18 September 2001; and the testimony of Brigadier Ivica Zeko in the ICTY trial of Tihomir Blaskic.
15. The presence in Bosnia of approximately 300 former Islamic fighters is also well documented. See, for example, Branko Peric, 'Bosnia and Terrorism', *AIM*, 27 September 2001, and 'Bin Laden and the Balkans: the Politics of Anti-Terrorism', International Crisis Group, 9 November 2001, p. 11.
16. Craig Pyesjosh Meyer and William C. Rempe, 'Bosnia: Bin Laden's Terrorist Base', *Los Angeles Times*, 7 October 2001; Drazen Simic, 'The Algerian Case', *AIM*, 25 January 2002; and Carol J. Williams, 'US Spirits 6 Terror Suspects Out of Bosnia', *Los Angeles Times*, 19 January 12002. Citing security concerns, the US closed its embassy in the Bosnian capital, Sarajevo, in March 2002.
17. Ibid.
18. Interview with author, Tirana, Albania, 8 February 2002. See also 'Former Security Head Says Albania Worked with Western Services against Terrorism', *Albania*, 21 September 2001; R. Jeffrey Smith, 'US Embassy Threatened in Albania', *Washington Post*, 15 August 1998; Christopher Cooper and Andrew Higgins, 'CIA-Backed Team Used Brutal Means to Crack Terror Cell', *Wall Street Journal*, 22 November 2001; Alan Cullison and Andrew Higgins, 'Computer Yields al Qaeda Memos', *Wall Street Journal Europe*, 2 January 2002; Hamza Hendawi, 'Confessions of Executed Militant in 1998 Trial Provide Insight into Terrorist Groups', Associated Press, 30 October 2001; and Susan Sachs, 'An Investigation in Egypt Illustrates Al Qaeda's Web', *New York Times*, 21 November 2001.
19. Christopher Cooper and Andrew Higgins, 'CIA-Backed Team Used Brutal Means to Crack Terror Cell', *Wall Street Journal*, 22 November 2001. Cooperation between SHIK and CIA was confirmed to the author in interviews with former and present Albanian government officials as well as with US officials.
20. The Albanian and international press has been rife with allegations and denials of Gazidede's ties to Islamic groups and the visit of bin Laden to Albania. See, for example, 'On the Trail of Bin Laden: Albania', *The Scotsman*, 21 September 2001; 'Paper: Suspected Top Terrorist Bin Laden

Visited Albania in 1984', Deutsche Presse Agentur, 4 November 1998; 'SHIK Said to Ignore CIA reports of Terrorists in Tirana', Albanian Telegraphic Agency, 3 June 1998; 'Former Security Head Says Albania Worked with Western Services Against Terrorism', *Albania*, 21 September 2001; and Colin Brown, 'Bin Laden Linked to Albanian Drug Gangs', *Independent*, 21 October 2001.

21. See, for example, R. Jeffrey Smith, 'US Embassy Threatened in Albania', *Washington Post*, 15 August 1998, and 'Bin Laden and the Balkans: the Politics of Anti-Terrorism', International Crisis Group, 9 November 2001, p. 5.

22. 'Former Security Head Says Albania Worked with Western Services against Terrorism', *Albania*, 21 September 2001.

23. 'Albania to Downgrade Relations with Islamic Countries', Deutsche Press Agentur, 5 December 1997.

24. Ibid.

25. Interviews with the author. See also Andi Bejtja, 'Islam, Albanians and War in Kosovo', *AIM*, 31 May 1999, and 'On the Trail of Bin Laden: Albania', *The Scotsman*, 21 September 2001.

26. 'Self-described Bin Laden Aide Convicted of Murder in Albania', *Dow Jones International News*, 14 November 1998, and 'Murder Defendant Tells of Bin Laden's Plans in Region', Albanian Telegraphic Agency, 7 November 1998.

27. Author's interview with former KLA member. This incident was also reported by the Yugoslav government and a newspaper owned by the federal government, although the two sources provided slightly different casualty numbers from each other and from the former KLA member interviewed by the author. See V.N., 'Strong Ties with the Mujahadin', *Vecernje Novosti*, 22 October 2001; D. Vujicic, 'Bin Laden's Camp in Kosovo', *Vecernje Novosti*, 26 September 2001; and 'Terrorism in Kosovo and Metohija—White Book', Yugoslav Ministry of Foreign Affairs, Belgrade, September 1998.

28. Author's interview with former KLA member.

29. Various articles in the Albanian and international press have covered this incident. The most detailed is Christopher Cooper and Andrew Higgins, 'CIA-Backed Team Used Brutal Means to Crack Terror Cell', *Wall Street Journal*, 22 November 2001.

30. Interview with author, Tirana, Albania, 8 February 2001.

31. R. Jeffrey Smith, 'US Embassy Threatened In Albania', *Washington Post*, 15 August 1998.

32. Christopher Cooper and Andrew Higgins, 'CIA-Backed Team Used Brutal Means to Crack Terror Cell', *Wall Street Journal*, 22 November 2001.

33. President William J. Clinton, 'Letter to Congressional Leaders Reporting on the Deployment of United States Forces to Protect the United States Embassy in Albania', 18 August 1998.

34. R. Jeffrey Smith, 'US Embassy Threatened in Albania', *Washington Post*, 15 August 1998.

35. Khaled Dawoud, 'Military Trial for Militant Suspects', *Al-Ahram Weekly*, 4–10 February 1999.

36. Jailan Halawi, '"Albanian Returnees" Executed', *Al-Ahram Weekly*, 2–8 March 2000.

37. Susan Sachs, 'An Investigation in Egypt Illustrates Al Qaeda's Web', *New York Times*, 21 November 2001; Khaled Dawoud, 'Military Trial for Militant Suspects', *Al-Ahram Weekly*, 4–10 February 1999; Christopher Cooper and Andrew Higgins, 'CIA-Backed Team Used Brutal Means to Crack Terror Cell', *Wall Street Journal*, 22 November 2001.
38. See Arjan Leka, 'Bin Laden Giving Albania a Headache', *AIM*, 26 September 2001.
39. For details on some of the steps taken by the Albanian government, see Arian Konomi, 'Albania in the Anti-Terrorist Coalition', *AIM*, 14 October 2001.
40. 'Albania No Longer a Refuge for Islamic Terrorists: Police Chief', Agence France Presse, 13 September 2001.
41. 'Abdul Wahab Bashir, 'Report about Albanian Arrest Warrant Denied', *Arab News*, 24 January 2002.
42. Abigail Levene, 'Milosevic Says FBI Paper Shows Al Qaeda in Kosovo', Reuters, 9 March 2002.
43. Peter Finn, 'Suspects in Macedonia Turned over to US', *Washington Post*, 7 March 2002; and Ana Petruseva, '"Mujahedin" Killings under Scrutiny', Institute for War and Peace Reporting, 8 March 2002.

References

Baker, James and DeFrank, Thomas. *The Politics of Diplomacy: Revolution, War and Peace: 1989–1992* (New York: G.P. Putnam's Sons, 1995).
Biberaj, Elez. *Albania in Transition: The Rocky Road to Democracy* (Boulder, Colorado: Westview Press, 1998).
Bejtja, Andi. 'Islam, Albanians and War in Kosovo', *AIM*, 31 May 1999.
Cooper, Christopher and Higgins, Andrew. 'CIA-Backed Team Used Brutal Means to Crack Terror Cell', *Wall Street Journal*, 22 November 2001.
Curtius, Mary. 'Baker Cheered as Hero in Albania', *Boston Globe*, 23 June 1991.
Fischer, Bernd. *Albania at War 1939–1945* (W. Lafayette: Purdue University Press, 1999).
Ford, Peter. 'Muslim Foreign Ministers Gather to Aid Bosnians', *Christian Science Monitor*, 1 December 1992.
Gardin, Giacomo. *Banishing God in Albania: The Prison Memoirs of Giacomo Gardin* (San Francisco: Ignatius Press, 1988).
International Crisis Group Report, 'Bin Laden and the Balkans: the Politics of Anti-Terrorism', 9 November 2001.
Leka, Arjan. 'Bin Laden Giving Albania a Headache', *AIM*, 26 September 2001.
Murphy, Carlyle. 'Fahd Urges Arms Raid for Bosnia', *Washington Post*, 2 December 1992.
Pettifer, James and Vickers, Miranda. *Albania: From Anarchy to a Balkan Identity* (New York: New York University Press, 1997).
Radin, Charles A. 'Bosnia Warns of Wider War at Islamic Parlay' *Boston Globe*, 18 June 1992.
Skeni, Stavro. *The Albanian National Awakening 1878–1912* (Princeton: Princeton University Press, 1967).
Sachs, Susan. 'An Investigation in Egypt Illustrates Al Qaeda's Web', *New York Times*, 21 November 2001.

6
Exploring Theoretical and Programmatic Changes in Contemporary Islamist Discourse: The Journal *Al-Manar al-Jadid*

Amr Hamzawy

Introduction

The first issue of the journal *Al-Manar al-Jadid* appeared in January 1998 in Cairo. The aim of its founders, including well-known Islamists such as Muhammad 'Imara, Tariq al-Bishri, 'Abd al-Wahhab al-Misiri, Yusuf al-Qaradawi and Rashid al-Ghanushi, as well as activists of the younger generation of the Islamist movement, e.g. Jamal Sultan and Kamal Habib, was 'to establish a civilised and authentic spiritual forum to combat the waves of westernization, arbitrariness and opportunism in the Islamic world. Those waves that currently seem to be raping the identity of the *Umma* and calling into question its historical foundations'.[1]

The link to the name of the periodical *Al-Manar* issued under the patronage of Rashid Rida in 1898 is given substance by the construction of an historical continuum from the situation of the *Umma* at the end of the nineteenth century to the state of the Islamic world at the threshold of the twenty-first century.

Rida already understood that the *Umma* required a new step forward into the future .... A new future, at whose horizon it would free itself from the heavy burden of stagnation, technological and scientific backwardness, and civilisatory sloth .... Today, at the end of the 20th century these hopes and fears are still on the agenda of most Arabic and Islamic societies.[2]

In the light of this analogy, the leading article written by Rida in 1898 and republished in the first issue of *Al-Manar al-Jadid* entitled

120

'*Risalat Al-Manar*' (The Message of *Al-Manar*) stands as a conceptual memorandum for the new journal. In addition to reviving Rida's version it was also the intention to take up the forgotten tradition of *islah* (reform) and *tajdid* (renewal), in which the early *Al-Manar* had stood, and to provide new impulses to move these to the centre of contemporary focus.[3] In other words, this involved drawing attention to the continuity and relevance of a religious discourse by means of a name with powerful symbolic resonance.[4]

The implied intention of showing the right way forward is reflected in the articles and essays in the first seven issues of the journal up to until October 2001. Under the heading 'Studies on religious philosophy and the state of society' topics were discussed such as the attitude of the Arabic-Islamic societies to the West and to western fashions, the threat of globalization, the roles of authenticity and renewal in current Islamic thought, the failure of nationalist and secular ideologies, the significance of religiously influenced educational systems and authentic forms of social organization, as well as the separation of religion and politics. However, this range of topics, which at first sight testifies to the continuation of well-known positions within the modern Islamist tendency, is accompanied by other essays which clearly indicate the beginning of a theoretical and programmatic transformation – particularly in terms of religious social criticism, the Islamic understanding of politics, the attitude to political rule and the necessity of dialogue with secular forces.

Before analysing the basic features of this change, I would like to comment on the authors and the thematic profile of *Al-Manar al-Jadid*.

First, a core group of 'Modernizers' has crystallized out from among the authors, belonging to both the moderate and radical wings of the Egyptian Islamists, but all members of the younger generation.[5] Prominent figures in this context are Jamal Sultan, editor-in-chief of the publication, Kamal Habib, journalist and a leading force in the 1980s in the Egyptian Jihad group and Husham Ja'far, member of the Egyptian Muslim Brotherhood. Within the contemporary Islamist movements they see their role as catalysts of a comprehensive process of intellectual and social reorientation. This is made clear in the regular editorial contributions (by Sultan) and various articles (by Habib and Ja'far), in which they attempt to draw 'lessons' from the experience of the Islamists over the past three decades. Here Sultan, Habib and Ja'far enjoy support from significant critical contributions from well-known Islamist thinkers such as al-Qaradawi and al-Ghanushi.

Second, the numerically strong representation of the Egyptian Islamists among the authors colours both the appearance and the content of the journal, and despite some contributions about the Islamist movements in other Arabic and Islamic societies, the 'pan-Islamic' claim of *Al-Manar al-Jadid* tends to be overshadowed by local Egyptian topics and debates.[6]

Third, in the case of a number of controversial topics, such as globalization, the new world order and the Islamization of knowledge, the published contributions to these debates often turn out to be little more than ideologically biased polemics, despite the claims of the editors and authors to objectivity. The multitude of world-wide processes involved in globalization are lumped together within the framework of a generalized perception and roundly condemned as a modern 'symbol' of ubiquitous western imperialism.[7] At the same time, many authors maintain that 'preserving' the achievements and special features of Islamic civilization, particularly in the face of the US-dominated new world order, will require an 'Islamization' of international relationships. In this context, terms such as *dar al-harb* (abode of war), *dar al-salam* (abode of peace) and *dar al-'ahd* (abode of the treaty) are transferred to the present as political science constructs in order to investigate the relationships between Islamic and non-Islamic countries. When such methods are presented as constituting the 'final results' of a five-year 'scientific' project, one can only wonder at the extent to which some Islamist thinkers have failed to understand contemporary realities.[8]

Fourth, it is notable that the term 'secular' is uniformly equated with 'irreligious'. This represents one element of a vehement criticism of western secular thought and its central premises in a number of articles in *Al-Manar al-Jadid*. The political scientist 'Abd al-'Aziz Saqr[9] claims that so-called 'secular state ideology' is nothing more than pure theory and Enlightenment myths. Religion has remained a constant pillar supporting political rule in the West since the Middle Ages.[10] In an emotional essay, 'Abd al-Wahhab al-Misiri[11] denounces western 'secular materialism' and contrasts it with 'humane, Islamic spirit'.[12] In particular, the introduction of secularism to the Arabic-Islamic area is condemned. A typical example of this is the comments of the Egyptian thinker Jalal Amin:[13] The so-called 'secular Enlightenment' in the Arab world amounts to little more than a campaign of hatred against Islam, while the 'arrogant' secular elite of thinkers and writers benefits in material terms from their intellectual rejection of Islam, because they find themselves courted in the West and by the 'irreligious' rulers of the Arabic-Islamic nation-states.[14] The style and content of these comments not only impy ideological polemics, but border on the outright defamation of non-Islamist intellectuals.[15]

Bearing these points in mind, we can now turn to our primary goal, namely an analysis of relevant essays and contributions to the journal *Al-Manar al-Jadid*, in order to determine the background and key elements of the apparent theoretical and programmatic change in the Islamist discourse. In order to set this in a broader context, the next section examines in some detail the essential features of the publication as seen by the editors and authors.

Four questions structure this study: 1) To what extent have the reactions to the successes and defeats of moderate and radical Islamist movements over the past three decades been the specific trigger for debates on change? 2) What reasons are given for the need for 'rethinking', and how is it justified religiously? 3) How is the change defined and what is the importance within this framework of the continuity in religious discourse to which the initiators of the journal attach so much importance? In short, what is the interaction between change and continuity? 4) What limitations arise from the 'continuity–change' dichotomy for the political and social attitudes of the Islamist movements?

The Essential Features of the Journal *Al-Manar al-Jadid*

When considering the origins of the journal it is possible to distinguish two points which reflect the goals of *Al-Manar al-Jadid*. First, to establish a new discussion forum for both external dialogue (between Islamists and other political and intellectual forces) and internal dialogue within Islamist discourse under *mawdu'iyya* (objectivity) and *hiyad* (neutrality).[16] Second, to revive the tradition of *islah* and *tajdid* in the Arabic-Islamic region, and thus bring about a 'moral transformation' in terms of Islam which is necessary in the opinion of the initiators of the journal, while working against the advanced 'alienation' of the *Umma* in all areas of life and society.[17]

The Establishment of a New Discussion Forum

Drawing attention to the financial independence of the journal in the editorial of the first issue, Jamal Sultan emphasizes that *Al-Manar* does not speak on behalf of any party or movement. Rather, it represents a 'spiritual forum which wishes to remain independent in both its message and its ambitions. The journal envisages an honest dialogue involving all lines of thought and approaches as the only way to enlightenment and renewal of the thought, the spirit and the will of the *Umma*. *Al-Manar al-Jadid* is convinced that responsible, serious and resolute pluralism provides proof of the health and vitality of the *Umma*. Therefore, the journal should 'be used in a fair dialogue to promote our thought in general and to search for the reasons for our misery, as well the search for the way to our re-awakening'.[18] The lack of exchange of ideas and of respect for the 'others' is seen by Sultan as a dominant negative feature of modern Arabic culture. In his opinion, pluralism and tolerance have been degraded to empty political slogans in the state-controlled media and secular forums, which nobody wishes to follow. *Al-Manar* can help here and provide a discussion forum for different intellectual and political movements within which the 'Arabic consciousness' can be enriched and the 'mentality of dependence' on the West can be opposed.[19]

However, in the second issue the editor-in-chief, writing under the promising heading 'The value of dialogue', expresses reservations which in part radically contradict the principles of pluralism and tolerance. To start with, Islam is presented as the sole common denominator for all the forces involved in the dialogue. Furthermore, the dialogue is set the onerous task of exposing the 'ignorance' of large sections of the irreligious intellectuals concerning Islamic history and traditions. Whether such a one-sided campaign can pave the way for a discussion with secular forces remains to be seen. Finally, the public, misled by state propaganda, should be informed about the 'true transgressions' of the corrupt, secular political elites.[20] The deliberate link between political matters (corruption) and social forces (the secular) considerably narrows the scope of the proposed dialogue. The exclusive character of these three premises thus undermines in advance the likelihood of any form of serious dialogue between Islamists and other movements in the Arabic-Islamic region.

The promotion of internal dialogue within Islamist discourse seems to stand in a different light. In this context the goal is to promote *fikr naqdi* (critical thought) regarding the evaluation of past experience and to clarify the future action strategies of the Islamists. On the other hand, a discussion is to be started about the shared values, differences and contradictions in the Islamist spectrum, in order, according to Sultan, to reduce the irrational fears of tactical compromise and pragmatic changes of direction.[21] As we will see below, *Al-Manar al-Jadid* is able to fulfil this task in exemplary fashion.

Reviving an Intellectual Tradition

Under the slogan *tajdid al-tajdid* (renewal of the renewal)[22] the founders of *Al-Manar al-Jadid* emphasize the significance of the religiously-based reform tradition in Arabic-Islamic societies and indicate the importance of reviving it. Two authors are taken as examples here, to investigate how variously accentuated historical analogies are constructed and how justifications relevant to the present times are articulated.

In order to recall the political and religious context of the old *Al-Manar*, the Egyptian thinker Muhammad 'Imara refers to the works of Jamal al-Din al-Afghani and Muhammad 'Abduh and the programmatic writings of Rashid Rida. 'Imara sees the efforts of the first reformers as an attempt to develop the fundamentals of a contemporary and civilizatory societal project in harmony with Islam, with intellectual horizons that call into question both the unthinking copying of the West and the uncritical following of the *salaf as-salih* (the forefathers). He refers to the dominant goals of the reform movement at the beginning of the twentieth century, which were to be supported by the journal *Al-Manar*, as: Opposing the 'harmful' western influence; formulating an authentic understanding of progress on the basis of the totality of Islam as religion, society and state; liberation of Islam from the *bid'a* (heretical teachings); publication of contemporary interpretations of the shari'a and socially relevant *fatawa* (legal opinions); mobilisation of the forces of renewal of the *Umma* with the support of public initiatives and associations; and finally, an emphasis on the gradual nature of reform in the Islamic tradition, in contrast to the contemporary secular views concerning the need for a radical break with the past.[23]

In view of the fact that after the death of Rida the founder of the Egyptian Muslim Brotherhood, Hassan al-Banna, took over the publication of *Al-Manar* from 1939 to 1940, 'Imara sees a continuity of history and content between the old reform tradition and the Muslim Brotherhood, which he regards as the first modern embodiment of the Islamist tendency.[24] He also broadens the boundaries of this continuity in order to include the mission of *Al-Manar al-Jadid* in an analogous framework. In his opinion, the initial goals remain important, given the unbroken dominance of the West, the continued stagnation of Arabic-Islamic societies and the intellectual marginalization of the reform tradition. With the help of the new publication, which follows in the tradition of its 'mother' and acts as the mouthpiece for the Islamists, the aim should be to renew the reform ideas and build these into a comprehensive social model.[25]

A similar, but more differentiated variant on the relevance of the reform tradition, taking Egypt as an example, is offered by the lawyer Tariq al-Bishri. He claims that westernization which has been in progress since the end of the nineteenth century has brought in its wake a radical separation between the irreligious, state elites and the religiously influenced common people. From then on, both 'true' Islamic thought and also democratic demands were confined to the sphere of authentic social institutions (*al-mujtama' al-ahli*). In his opinion, it was in this context that the movement of Islamic renewal developed, which, although in the theological sense it only involved an adaptation of the legal opinions to a changed reality, incorporated two goals – stemming the influx of western influences and opposing secular tendencies. The 'struggle' against the ruling elites, however, restricted the chances that reform projects such as the journal *Al-Manar* would survive. In addition, according to al-Bishri, the West-oriented, elitist projects in the political and social fields received more support from the irreligious state.[26]

Regarding western influences, al-Bishri distinguishes three areas. In law a new legal system was established outside the rules and norms of Islamic law. At the intellectual level, a new educational system was oriented towards the tenets of western science and arts so that theological subjects were eliminated from 'modern' curricula. Finally, European lifestyles and secular codes of behaviour were increasingly copied in daily life.[27] As a result of these developments, the renewal movement sought to 'expose harmful westernization', but could not avoid confronting the reasons for the backwardness of the Arabic-Islamic societies:

> Islamic thought saw itself confronted with two central tasks which at first sight indicate an internal contradiction. One goal was to defend the fundamentals of Islamic religion as a basis for social order, the social norms and attitudes as well as individual behaviour. This presupposes the preservation of the foundations

of belief against threats from outside. On the other hand it was also manifestly necessary to renew thought and to organise the society more rationally and efficiently ...[28]

Whereas the first task involved holding on to fundamentals, the second demanded mental flexibility and freedom to experiment with regard to religious principles. The conflict between the conservative scholars in the *al-Azhar* institution and the reformers of *Al-Manar* at the end of the nineteenth century represents in his view an expression of the duality of continuity and change.

Nevertheless, al-Bishri claims that the gap between the conservative and reformist tendencies has narrowed since the end of the First World War as a result of convergence. This is based, on the one hand, on broad recognition of the reform approach of al-Afghani, 'Abduh and Rida on the part of the *Azhar* institution and the religiously motivated movements, above all the Muslim Brotherhood. Following this, the works of the three thinkers became an essential base for the 'Islamic involvement' in all social spheres. On the other hand, the interest of the *Azhar* scholars, namely an emphasis on the totality of Islam as *din wa dunya* (i.e. covering both faith and life issues) was accepted in the context of the reform efforts. The convergence of both tendencies of Islamic thought, according to al-Bishri, included an overall orientation to Islam and an end for the time being to the disputes about the standing of conservatism and renewal.[29] But at this point he fails to provide his readers with concrete information about the future importance of his statements. The question concerning the limits and difficulties of the real programmatic implementation of the historical compromise between conservatives and reformers of the religious spectrum is not discussed. The overall development of the Islamist discourse in the twentieth century, from the idea of renewal, through the propagation of social upheaval, to the support of violence, is not a part of his considerations.

After proposing a sort of United Islamic Front, al-Bishri turns to concentrate on the conflict between secular and religious movements. Despite the common overriding goal of national independence, the two camps of secular nationalists and Islamically influenced reformers had been divided since the 1920s regarding the future form of society and the political attitude. Whereas secular thinkers and politicians envisaged the separation of state and religion, the Islamist groups favoured the establishment of a social system oriented towards the principles of shari'a. National independence in 1954 did nothing to reduce the controversy about the future of Egypt; on the contrary it led to an escalation. In this context, al-Bishri passes a crushing but generalized verdict on the secular experiments, both liberal (1923–52) and socialist (1956–70):

> The failure of the liberal and socialist attempts led to a radical change in the national consciousness of Egypt. Because the modern nation discovered Islam and began to cling to it as the true identity of its existence. At the same time the admiration for social models of western origin declined.[30]

On the basis of this he claims that there has been a theoretical and programmatic shift in the direction of Islamist efforts since the 1970s. The changes made the religious forces more self-confident and this was reflected in a new edge to their social criticism and their reform strategies. As the confrontation with the secularists became less important, the Islamists could increasingly turn their attention to the realization of their own goals. For al-Bishri this is the reason for the current variety of interests and fields of activity, the political methods used and the groups targeted by the Islamists. In his opinion, this phase represents a unique opportunity to develop a new, contemporary compromise in the Islamist understanding of politics and society between the central fundamentals of conservation and reform. And it is precisely in this context that he attempts to anchor the new journal *Al-Manar al-Jadid*. This has the task of increasing the discussion potential in the religious movements by providing critical and unconventional impulses.[31]

Considered together, the analyses of 'Imara and al-Bishri provide an intellectualized discourse, the coordinates of which can be appreciated only in light of their understanding of history and the analytical extraction of significant changes in the Arabic-Islamic area. On the one hand, the claims concerning a 'stagnation' of the *Umma* since the end of the nineteenth century reflect a one-sided interpretation of historical developments as a history of decadence (*inhitat*) and the departure from the fundamentals (unity of God and *Umma*) of a religiously idealized Golden Age – an interpretation that is frequently encountered in the modern Islamist historiography.[32] On the other hand, the authors are able to ignore completely the real processes of change ('*Imara*) or to present these in broad and sometimes idiosyncratic outline (al-Bishri). Instead, more attention is paid to the possibility of the 'restoration' of the Golden Age, in connection with *Al-Manar al-Jadid* by means of the revival of a reform tradition as a magic solution for all problems. The same understanding of history can be found regarding the evaluation of the progress of contemporary Islamist schools of thought: the current moderate significance of the reform idea and the radicalization of Islamic movements since the 1960s are seen as an internal fall from the tradition of *islah* and *tajdid*, a situation that is to be redressed with the help of the new publication.

It is possible to deduce from this that the notions of continuity and change in the discussions of 'Imara and al-Bishri have two central connotations: the persistence of decadence as a general tendency in human societies and the desirable return to an idealized moment in Islamic history. The notion of change is relevant in this context only as an embodiment of the transition from the decadence to the restoration of the idealized times (early Islamic phase) or as a symbol of the rediscovery of a religiously appropriate approach (reform tradition). The change is defined in terms of continual reference to past moments and thus loses its future-oriented substance. This represents the retrogressive aspect of the continuity–change dichotomy in the discussions of the journal *Al-Manar al-Jadid*.

However, there remains sufficient scope beneath this general level to attach other connotations to the notions of continuity and change in contemporary Islamist discourse and thus to oppose the limitations of this aspect of the dichotomy. The fact that some of the authors in *Al-Manar al-Jadid* make use of this freedom leads to an extension of the term 'changeable' in the current Islamist spectrum, as will be shown in the next section, so that it is possible to speak of a theoretical and programmatic renewal.

The Causes and Key Pillars of the Theoretical and Programmatic Change in the Islamist Discourse

The editorial goal of conducting an open dialogue between the various religiously influenced groups about their experience over the past three decades and their ideas for the future concerning the relationship to political rule and the social role of the Islamists is followed by the majority of the authors in the selected issues of *Al-Manar al-Jadid*. Two viewpoints can be distinguished. The first subjects the strategies and approaches adopted by Islamists since the 1970s to critical scrutiny; the second involves a debate on the so-called 'teachings of the past' (*'ibar al-madi*) and the prospects of theoretical and programmatic renewal in Islamist thought.

Within this framework, the process of rethinking is legitimized by emphasizing the overall societal changes and the diversity of experiences in the Islamic world in the twentieth century. In other words, the primacy of continuity, which is central to the revival of the reform tradition, is replaced by a dynamic perception of the reality of modern Arabic-Islamic societies and a pragmatic placing of the phenomenon of Islamism in their horizons. This does not represent a contradiction in the discourse of *Al-Manar al-Jadid*, but rather marks a necessary shift of focus in the discussion towards the inclusion of time-related factors, with which the essential nature of a future-oriented reform can be demonstrated. Thus while the link to the past within the 'continuity–change' dichotomy remains the central legitimizing paradigm of the Islamist thought, it is qualified by a link to the contemporary, and thus freed in part from its own limitations, while remaining intact as the central paradigm of Islamist thought.

Disorientation, Neglect of Moral Considerations, Increased Militarization and the Acceptance of Violence: On the Fallibility of Islamism

Thanks to the contributions of well-known thinkers and scholars, the critical review of the successes and failures of Islamism develops into a fundamental discussion of the definition, justification, goals and ideal characteristics of religiously influenced movements in the contemporary Arabic-Islamic context. The various degrees of emphasis placed on the fundamentals of Islamism then determine the extent to which the strategies and activities of these movements over the past three decades are viewed retrospectively as conformist or as misguided.

The Tunisian scholar Rashid al-Ghanushi defines the mass phenomenon of Islamism as the 'sum of the individual and collective efforts of numerous faithful men and women in order to lead Muslims back to their merciful God'.[33] Based on Islam as the only true source of orientation, the Islamists have the duty to start a process of re-Islamization in all spheres of life by means of legal and educational reforms, and thus to make it possible to realize a model of society and politics based on the authentic principles of *shura* and *siyasa shar'iyya*.[34]

The relevance of contemporary Islamism is felt by al-Ghanushi to lie in the vitality and uniqueness of its role. This is based on the widespread view held in Islamist thought that the historical transformation initiated a radical break in the continuity of Islamic history: The rise of modern nation-states in the Arabic-Islamic area was followed by the end of the classical separation of power between rulers and religious scholars, which was based on a functional distinction between the spheres of politics and society. In their traditional double role, the scholars legitimized despotic rule (as long as its representatives respected the shari'a in all aspects of society and continued to allow scholars access to the masses), while at the same time they protected the people from repression and despotic excesses by systematically limiting the scope of politics. However, this lost its significance in the national context. The new national elites, true to their authoritarian views, rejected the participation of any other forces in the formation of the 'new society'. They degraded religious institutions to nationalized instruments helping them to preserve their own power and adopted the religious contents and symbols for their own secular goals. According to al-Ghanushi, the scholars could either obey the rulers and thus ensure minimum freedoms (in the educational sphere in particular) or form opposition groups to act against the absolutist nation-state and preserve the 'free spirit' of the *Umma*. The Egyptian Muslim Brotherhood, the oldest manifestation of Islamism, embodied the implementation of the second option, and with the works of Hassan al-Banna and Sayyid Qutb paved the way for the development of numerous other movements in the Arabic-Islamic area which did not recognize the power of the nation-state and which endeavoured with reformist (pacifist) and radical means to replace it with an Islamic state.[35]

Although al-Ghanushi continues to regard the goal of the Islamist movements to establish a *dawla islamiyya* (an Islamic state) as essential, he emphasizes that the painful experiences of the past three decades make it necessary to reassess the strategies used and examine their conformation with Islamic values and norms as well as their political effectiveness. The radical and violent approach characteristic of many attempts to bring about change in the 1980s and 1990s is in stark contrast to the authentic concept of gradual change in Islamic thought. Such attempts damaged the *Umma* as well as the credibility of the Islamists, the majority of whom have come to see in recent years that violence was no alternative and that a complete rejection of modern social structures offered no real prospects for the future. He therefore pleads for a rejection of the militant paradigm of Sayyid Qutb and for a 'return' to the reform tradition of al-Afghani, 'Abduh and Rida, above all to the pacifist, ethical-moral principles of al-Banna. In the approach of the first reformers, al-Ghanushi sees the specification of the longing of Muslims for gradual ethical and social change which takes account of the 'universal *Zeitgeist'* while also establishing in the present the characteristic Islamic forms of society and politics.

By concentrating on the three aspects – 'gradualism', '*Zeitgeist'* and 'bringing into the present' – as criteria for the evaluation of social activities, al-Ghanushi creates considerable scope for relativizing some Islamist premises which have been sacrosanct since the 1970s. For example, he asks to what extent the traditional scepticism against establishing political parties, which can be traced back to the old debate about *hizbiyya,* can still be maintained in today's context. In view of the split in the Islamist spectrum and the minimal degree of coordination between the various movements, in his opinion the integrating structure of political parties could certainly prove very beneficial.[36]

On the basis of his experience in the Jihad group, Kamal Habib continues to question the current Islamist understanding of the political. He notes that the first phase of the 'Islamist revival' in Egypt between 1967 and 1981 had three central characteristics. First, the founding generation of members were revolutionary students who rejected the secular Nasserite state and felt that they had to break with the conformist attitude of the Muslim Brotherhood. Second, the works of Ibn Taymiyya and Sayyid Qutb represented the source of inspiration for the Islamist student groups. Whereas the guiding principle of Ibn Taymiyya's *qital al-ta'ifa al-mumtani'a* had provided the main religious justification for the use of violence against the unjust ruler, by describing the Nasserite regime as *nizam jahili* (a regime of ignorance), Qutb makes it possible to see the legislative, executive and judiciary structures of the Egyptian state as Godless and therefore a justifiable target of violent struggle. Taking this further, Habib writes that the social order at that time was seen by the Islamists as an antithesis of the true Islamic system, so that it had to be replaced.

Third, the classic distinction in Islamic jurisprudence between the constant and changing elements of religion was not taken into consideration. As a result, Habib saw a cognitive unification of moral-ethical and social elements of Islam crystallizing, leading to an increasingly dogmatic attitude towards social and political forms. As an example, he cites the ideas of Islamist students, including some in his group, to re-establish the early Islamic structures, in particular the 'khilafa' (Caliphate) system.[37]

Habib's interpretation of the developments in the 1980s sheds light on two chains of events. Following the murder of al-Sadat and due to the abandonment by the government of most of its de-escalation policies towards the moderate and radical Islamists, the influence of militant student groups visibly spread beyond the confines of the universities, giving rise to two important movements, al-jama'a al-islamiyya and the Jihad-group. At the same time, the moderation and reform of the Muslim Brothers seemed less and less attractive in the Islamist spectrum. Their activities within the political channels allowed by the government were regarded as ineffective and in the end as providing legitimization for the state. Violence seemed to be able to establish itself as the only means of change.[38]

The subsequent escalation between the regime and the radical movements into the 1990s, and the 'senseless' spiral of violence and counter-violence are viewed by Habib in terms of their negative effects on the overall development of Islamism. First, the Islamists became increasingly alienated from society and were seen by the majority as the instigators of the violence. Second, intellectual immobility crept into the Islamist spectrum leading to a lack of ideas and preventing any attempt to draw on other sources beyond the works of Ibn Taymiyya and Sayyid Qutb, or to articulate new strategies. In his opinion, the radical movements lost contact with their original egalitarian structures, oriented towards the shura principle. A process of internal militarization began, in the course of which he sees many activists losing their 'mental health'.[39]

In addition, Habib introduces another aspect in his criticism of the Islamist view of politics. Following al-Ghanushi, he draws attention to the importance of distinguishing between the moral-ethical and the political ideals of Islam. Whereas the former are immutable and universal, in his opinion the interpretation of the latter depend on the subjective understanding of the individual scholar and the social situation in any given historical context. From this he derives, for example, the temporal dependence of the implementation of the important hakimiyya principle (rule of God). The establishment of an Islamic state represents merely the form of realization of the religious ideal, and its current plausibility must be examined. It is therefore not possible to exclude *a priori* the relevance of other models, such as a democratic state with broadly Islamic features.

A similar relativist approach is applied when evaluating the views of Ibn Taymiyya and Qutb on the justifications for the use of force. Habib feels that both authors produced their work in 'exceptional' phases of Islamic history. The brutal negation of Islam by the Tatars and Nasserism had justified the consideration of violence as an option in the struggle against an unjust ruler.[40] In his opinion, the special character of these two moments meant that it was not possible to generalize for all eras. For the most part, the kings and presidents exercising political power today in the Arabic-Islamic area could neither be accused of lack of knowledge nor lack of belief. This historical argument is then followed by a more practical consideration. He argues that the scope for using violence successfully against a ruler depends on the balance of power and the ability of the rebel group in question to oppose the ruler. The current experience of the Islamists shows that the militant struggle against the modern authoritarian nation-state has no hope of success, and will bring only sacrifices and loss to all parties. Taking both the historical and political components into consideration, Habib pleads for a general rejection of the use of violence and a new political start for the Islamists in the sense of the revival of the reformist thought of Rida's *Al-Manar*.[41]

The tension between the gradual and radical views of change in the Islamist views of society and politics, with its discursive and real implications, is studied by the Egyptian political scientist Husham Ja'far in terms of the opposing concepts of 'dominance of religion over politics' and 'domination of politics over religion'. The Islamic involvement is based in his opinion on the attempt to transfer religious visions to politics and thus to establish a moral influence over its structures and content. In view of the differing characters of religion and politics this can become problematic. Whereas Islamic regulations are absolute, politics represents the sphere of the historical, the changing, the pragmatic and the pluralistic. Religious dominance over politics which takes account of the constant transformations in the political field is only possible under the premise of relativity regarding the implementation of religious ideals and tolerance towards other views. The parliamentary and extra-parliamentary activities of the Muslim Brotherhood in countries such as Egypt and Jordan are seen as one possible approach by Ja'far. In contrast, in his opinion, the increased influence of politics in religion, above all by radical movements, leads to increased dogmatism. Politics is no longer the art of the possible and the search for compromise, but an expression of the imposition of a certain interpretation of the religious ideals, which are declared as infallible on the strength of a claimed monopoly of truth. He sees a growing sacralization of the political, taking place outside the historical sphere.[42]

The effects of this in the opinion of Ja'far are fatal. At the level of discourse the unhistorical view of politics has led to a fixation within the radical spectrum on the seizure of political power as the sole means of change. The general social crisis in the Arabic-Islamic area is interpreted as a crisis of the irreligious state, which must be eliminated if the crisis is to be overcome. In this context, the programmatic writings of 'Abd al-Salam Faraj (*al-farida al-gha'iba*) and Salih Sariyya (*risalat al-iman*) were in his opinion the clearest outcome of the modern intellectual production. The dominance of the political had an even more negative effect within the radical discourse on the standing of the moral and ethical contents, which were revalued and marginalized. A two-sided process began, with neglect of the moral considerations and an increase in political influence in religion, leading to estrangement between the militant movements and their religious surroundings. At the practical level, Ja'far, like Habib and others before him, complains of the rigidity and ignorance about current political affairs. The loss of links to the contemporary while holding on to outdated views, for example the accusation that society and state are Godless, reflects, in the final analysis, the failure of radical Islamism.[43]

Jamal Sultan rounds off the critical evaluation with three remarks from the realm of *realpolitik*. First, the readiness of radical groups to use violence has stimulated the despotic dreams of some leaders and thus led to the formation of authoritarian structures in which loyalty to the *amir* (leader of the group) and his interpretation of Islam replaces the orientation to the 'overall goals of Islamism' as a reference system. A leadership cult with a religious slant was established, followed by a sometimes brutal process of elimination of critical activists and nonconformists. Blind obedience to the leader, even transgressing the rules and ideals of Islam, was reflected in the numerous excesses in the context of the confrontation with the regime. As examples of barbaric actions, Sultan cites the murder of nonconformist intellectuals and the targeted use of violence against religious minorities, which could not possibly be justified by a 'true' understanding of Islam. Second, the majority of the radical Islamists see the state as a homogeneous unit which can be changed only by means of a total seizure of power. Any suggestions of transformation and reform were rejected as collaboration with the existing power structures, and their proponents were severely criticized within the Islamist spectrum. The reason for this, according to Sultan, lies in the lack of any form of historical consciousness and an undifferentiated view of political developments. This gave rise to actions that set themselves above the 'conditions of reality' and were counterproductive regarding the achievement of the primary goal of all Islamists, the gradual moral transformation in accordance with Islam. Instead of collective salvation in the long term, there was a glorification of the radical and of martyrdom, which manifested itself in meaningless operations. Looking to the future, Sultan concludes that the tide of violence is beginning to ebb, and that the self-defined goals have not been reached. But the radical movements had not gained power, nor had the nation-states of the Arabic-Islamic area been seriously destabilized, with the exception of Algeria. He sees the first signs of renouncing violence in the numerous initiatives since 1997 in which radical Islamists have declared their commitment to non-violence,[44] but he emphasizes that this trend needs to be backed up by a theoretical and programmatic renewal of Islamist thought, which inevitably must orient itself on the premises of the old reform tradition, as al-Ghanushi defines them.[45]

A number of analytical conclusions can be drawn from the various facets of the internal criticism of the radical Islamist views presented here: the plea for a return to the gradual reform tradition and to the ethical-moral beginnings of modern Islamism does indeed mark a break with the dominance over the past three decades of the writings of Ibn Taymiyya and Qutb, which are seen by the authors to have failed, and to be ahistorical and/or estranged from reality. Whereas since the 1970s such negative judgements have generally been a central element of secular criticism of the phenomenon of Islamism, their adoption by some Islamic thinkers and activists marks the beginning of a profound change in their discourse. The radical understanding of the relationship between religion and society was previously based on the assumption that social structures would have to be formed anew in terms of an essentialized, religious world picture. The consideration of historical and contemporary processes of change when determining the objective of Islamism represents a reversal of the one-sided understanding of the dialectic of religion and society. The question of the social plausibility of certain religious contents and the way these are presented therefore has an orientational relevance. This process can be interpreted as an inner secularization of the religious discourse in the sense of adaptation to existing social realities.[46]

The persistent use of the terms 'return' and 'beginnings' can be interpreted here as an attempt to justify the adaptation by emphasizing a conceptual and symbolic affinity to the old reform tradition and thus to the main, backward-looking paradigm of Islamist thought. The call to rediscover the ethical-moral dimensions of Islamism represents a provisional response to the immanent tension between continuity and change. By restoring[47] the separation between timeless (ethical-moral) and changing (socially related) elements of Islam, the sacral character of the former are emphasized, as is their liberation from the transient secular constraints of social developments. In other words, the authors treated here see a move away from the politicization of religion, which threatened to bring about a complete secularization of Islam.[48] The (re)sacralization of moral-ethical principles means that these will be taken out of the sphere of politics, at least in part, and will in future fulfil the function of stabilizing the Islamist reference system. The Islamic understanding of politics can thus be freed from the limitations of the dichotomy between retrogression and adaptation. A contemporaneous sphere arises within Islamist thought, with religiously legitimized boundaries, within which the theoretical and programmatic dimensions of the involvement of Islamist movements in society can be renewed.

Fiqh al-waqi' *and* Fiqh al-taghyir: *Pillars of the Theoretical and Programmatic Renewal within the Islamist Discourse*

Within the incipient theoretical renewal, some main trends can be identified. The Egyptian scholar Yusuf al-Qaradawi living in the United Arab Emirates, argues for the integration of the Islamist understanding of politics in the theoretical framework of *siyasa shar'iyya* (politics reflecting Islamic law). He sees this as the 'contemporary interpretation of the partial interests of people in the context of the holistic goals of faith' and sets it on one level with the legal teaching of the experienced reality (*fiqh al-waqi' al-mu'ash*). According to him, this teaching is based on 'an objective, scientific treatment of reality and its changed elements',[49] with the aim of realizing the general religious ideals in different societal spheres. It takes place with the inclusion of spatial change (from society to society) and changes over time in the contextualization of *fatawa*. Such a process of examination and, if necessary, revision of religious judgements is in the opinion of al-Qaradawi more necessary than ever in an age of rapid and profound transformations.[50]

In addition, the acceleration of processes of social change in the Arabic-Islamic area makes it necessary to formulate a new jurisprudence, what al-Qaradawi terms *fiqh al-taghyir* (jurisprudence of change). He summarizes its theological foundations with three principles of religious thought. Taking account of human necessities, tolerating the lesser of two evils, and the gradual nature of change. Whereas the first principle stands for the orientation towards distinctive social, economic and political features when reaching religious judgements affecting a particular society, the other two represent the *de facto* exclusion of radical change as an option for change in accordance with Islam. The differentiation of social transgressions and the emphasis on the gradual progression towards religious ideals permit only a long-term approach to reform which takes account of the historical dimension of societal transformations. As an example, al-Qaradawi cites the scope for the application of the shari'a in the Egyptian context. The secular legal system adopted in colonial times is a transgression from an Islamic point of view, but it is crucial for the functioning of many vital spheres. In order not to destabilize the society, its justifiable replacement is only practically possible by a gradual and partial implementation of the provisions of the shari'a. In this way, an important objective of Islamist thought is subordinated under the reality of the situation, but also under the higher priority in the *fiqh* of protecting the interests of the people. This should in no way be seen, according to al-Qaradawi as a religiously justified delaying tactic, but as the embodiment of the gradual essence of the message of Islam.[51]

A second area of reform is considered by Kamal Habib. He discusses the state form and the importance of parliamentary elections as two aspect of the Islamist view of democracy. Regarding the state form, he notes that neither the characteristics of an Islamic state nor the means by which it is to be erected are determined by divine law. Therefore, it is the task of Muslims today to develop their subjective ideas based on both the overall goals of Islam and on the reality in which they are living. In this respect the ideals that are reflected in the utopia of the Islamic state count for more than the adherence to essentialized experience or rigid forms.[52] In the view of Habib, the acceptance of pluralistic principles of modern democracy, and the increasing willingness of many Islamist movements to take part in parliamentary elections in order to implement political reforms in accordance with Islam, can be interpreted as a contemporary strategy to realize some of those ideals. The religious legitimization of such a vision, as long as its adherents see it as a potentially fallible form of *ijtihad*, is anchored within the framework of the interpretative freedom of religious politics.[53]

A further theoretical tenet draws on the proposal to return to the ethical-moral and pacifist beginnings of Islamism in the twentieth century. Al-Qaradawi, Habib and al-Ghanushi see the need to turn away from an obsession with the politics of the past three decades and rediscover the social and cultural dimensions of society as a whole. In the tradition of the old *Al-Manar* they favour concentrating Islamist efforts on social and cultural areas, so that the fundamentals of the Islamic reform can be established – the moral re-education of the individual and the articulation of a moral-ethical civilizatory project.

However, the concentration on society, which Habib describes as 'post-politics' (*ma ba'd al-siyasa*), does not involve abandoning all political involvement, but rather revaluating politics in the Islamist discourse. This represents only one partial area of the range of action of Islamism, but one which, due to the realities of Arabic-Islamic societies, invariably leads to confrontation with political authorities. Learning ways to deal gradually with political constraints and the articulation of a tolerant view of politics is therefore possible only in intermediary social and cultural spaces between the state-controlled official politics and the individual sphere. The variety of the experience and the patterns of interaction in those areas in which the Islamists are well represented, thanks to the historical depth of their message, allows the movements to become acquainted with the pluralist features of modern civil societies (al-Ghanushi) and to revive tolerance towards other schools of thought which is rooted in the Islamic citizens' society (Habib).[54]

On the basis of the differentiation in Islamist political thought between religious ideals and the form of their realization, the emphasis on the need for contemporary interpretation of both elements of religious politics, and the notion of post-politics, a number of profound programmatic guides to action are being developed for Islamic movements in the Arabic-Islamic region, as has been indicated above. In summary, they can be expressed as follows. First, strict non-violence, irrespective of the attitude of the state in question or the animosity of other political forces. Second, legitimization of Islamist political parties, as a means of gradually transporting religious ideals into politics.[55] Third, an end to the instrumentalization in public of questions of belief and accusations of apostasy, as an expression of the partial withdrawal of moral-ethical elements of Islam from the public realm.[56] Fourth, active, pluralist participation in the social and cultural organizations and activities in the modern society in the conviction that this represents the most promising strategy for gradual reform in accordance with Islam.[57]

Epilogue

Thanks to a core group of modernizers, the analysis of the experience of the Islamic movements over the past three decades in the journal *Al-Manar al-Jadid* has led to a comprehensive renewal of the religiously influenced understanding of politics and society. The backward-looking character of the idea of renewal, which is reproduced by the construction of variously accentuated affinities to idealized moments of the past, should not obscure the significance of the theoretical and programmatic changes in the Islamist discourse. The repeated reversion to authentic experiences (early Islamic period) and traditions (reform tradition of the early *Al-Manar*) is revalued and reduced to the functionality of stabilizing the sacral reference system and the legitimization of renewal. Thus new space is created in Islamist thought for a discourse in which, taking account of religious ideals and historical transformations, answers can be developed for the problems immanent to all religious discourse – between retrogression and adaptation, between the demands for continuity and the need for change. The variety of answers proposed and the vitality of the discussions in *Al-Manar al-Jadid*, which I have attempted to present above, leave the author and interested readers grateful for the originality of scholars (al-Qaradawi and al-Ghanushi) and the forthright self-criticism of far-sighted activists (Habib and Ja'far).

These critical tendencies, however, have been only partially demonstrated in the course of Islamist intellectual accounts of the September 11 attacks and their underlying causes. In general, readers of Arab daily or weekly newspapers were either confronted with stereotypical and ideologically influenced articles about Islamism and the relationship of the Arab world towards the West, usually accentuating the US support of radical Islamist groups in the 1980s and 1990s and criticizing the general western policy with regard to the Arab-Islamic world, or articles that emphasize the peaceful nature of Islam and the faulty theses of Samuel P. Huntington about the clash of civilizations and world religions. Even though most of the contributions to this subject were written by renowned Islamists, the internal and regional factors causing the emergence of radical ideologies and movements were rarely discerned and discussed. Criticism of the West was voiced with such frequency and obvious disregard of the context, that one comes to the conclusion that, although a fundamental condemnation of the September 11 attacks prevailed, an indirect justification simultaneously underlay the perception of these events, in the sense of 'it serves you right'. The supposed secret approval of the attacks and bin Laden's popularity among the Arab peoples were explained by his willingness to deal with significant problems (e.g. Palestine) and his ability to teach the 'arrogant Americans' a lesson. The character of bin Laden, which several Islamists were creating, is in many senses reminiscent of that created for Saddam Hussein during the second Gulf War. Even though the differences between their respective discourses and goals were highlighted, Osama bin Laden was portrayed with the same aura of a local hero.

The fear of the cultural consequences of globalization and the supposed loss of authentic identity were becoming central arguments in the justification for the struggle against the imperialistic West. It has been claimed as the only remaining possibility to save the threatened Arab-Islamic world from Christian colonial rulers. It is another indirect way of legitimizing Islamist violence, however now in terms of an authenticated identity context.

A subsequent component was added to these central lines of argumentation: the conspiracy theories. They can be differentiated in terms of three basic patterns of perception. The first asserts that US intelligence orchestrated the September 11 attacks, with the intention of justifying an already planned general attack on the Arab and Islamic *Umma*. A second group of conspiracy theorists claims that the Christian Occident, characterized by religious hatred, intended to rid the West of its Muslim residents by demonstrating fanaticism on their part. This second theory seemed to be confirmed by the apparent smear campaigns against Islam in parts of the western media and the first legal steps taken against active Islamist groups in Europe. The use of the symbolic term 'crusade' by the US president not only served conspiracy theorists as proof of western hatred of Islam, but also emphasized the link they see between current US policy and negative historical experiences between the Orient and the Occident. The third variation of conspiracy theories mostly appears in Arab journal articles. It assumes that: the western world, dominated by international Zionism and the Israeli state, carried out the terrorist attacks under the leadership of Israeli intelligence, in order to justify the brutal behaviour of the Israeli Administration against Palestinians in the Occupied Territories. To this effect, the rumour claiming all Jewish employees of the World Trade Center were mysteriously absent on September 11, was circulated and widely accepted as true. This last variation of conspiracy theories represents a return to the most frequently used explanation of crisis situations by the Arab public: 'it's the Jews' fault'. Whether it be the gradual spread of the HIV virus in the Arab region (allegedly by female Israeli HIV-positive intelligence agents who deliberately seduce Arab men in order to infect them) or the poor cotton harvest in Egypt (due to modified seeds supplied by the Israeli government), Israel is always the culprit.

A prime example illustrating how these different theories, regarding conspiracies against the Arab world and Islam, do not necessarily exclude one another, is the 3 November article of the renowned Egyptian Islamist Mustafa Mahmud in the Egyptian daily newspaper *Al-Ahram*. Mahmud accuses the West of having planned its crusade against Islam over several decades. The terrorist attacks of September 11, which, according to Mahmud, were carried out by American groups, served as a justification for an attack on an innocent nation, the Islamic *Umma*. In his opinion, the increasing brutality of the Israeli army against Palestinians is not only an expression of the current anti-Islamic attitude shown by the Jewish state, but also proof of Israel's participation in these attacks. In an apocalyptic manner, the war in Afghanistan is claimed to be the last stand between true Islam and the materialistic civilization of the West. Thus, this emphasis on the Islamic We-community with its continual anguish shown through martyrdom, and the promised downfall of the West, do not only elucidate a radical Islamist interpretation of the end of history. It rather completes the last circle of an Islamist variation of messianic thought, in which goodness and its hero (in this case bin Ladin) ultimately prevail.[58]

Aside from such simplified and equivocal explanations, a fairly small number of critical articles represented important critical ideas. For example, both the Lebanese philosopher Ridwan as-Sayyid and the Egyptian al-Misiri related their defence of 'true Islam' to a critique of radical Islamism and its perception of politics and society. Both condemned a simplified depiction of Islamic politics as merely the implementation of the shari'a and the readiness to use force as a means of Islamizing contemporary Arab societies. At the same time, they refused to legitimize the terrorist attacks by simultaneously pointing to US foreign policy over the last few decades in relation to the Middle East.[59]

Even though these critical ideas and works still do not assume a central position in the Islamist treatment of the September 11 events and their consequences, they bear great potential for the future. Both the possible intellectual isolation of radical Islamism on the one hand, and the public discussion of the normative underpinnings of modern Arab societies on the hand, are significant aspects to continue observing. My impression is that September 11 has shaken some Arab Islamist thinkers and writers awake. It is becoming increasingly difficult to explain our crises in relation to the evil West and thus divert attention from our own failures. Ironically, this might be a significant step forward in the dialogue between the Orient and the Occident.

Notes

1. Sultan (1998a: 4).
2. Ibid., p. 5.
3. Ibid., pp. 5–6.
4. Quoted from al-Bishri (1998: 23–4).
5. A frequently used identification category is '*jil al-sab'ina't* [Generation of the 1970s]. Quoted from Sha'ban (1999: 76–85); Iskandar (1999: 96–106); Rumih (1998: 68–75).
6. Khalifa (1998: 18–38); Harb (1998: 105–12); al-'Arabi (1999: 35–41).
7. 'Amru Abd al-Karim, 'Al-'aulama: 'alam thalith 'ala abwab qarn jadid', *Al-Manar al-Jadid*, No. 3, Summer 1998, pp. 32–45; al-Sharif (1999: 8–24).
8. Quoted from Tammam (1998: 129–35).
9. Professor at the University of Cairo.
10. Quoted from Saqr (1998: 39–48) and Saqr (1999: 48–64).
11. Professor Emeritus for English Studies (University of 'Ayn Shams) and author of the controversial 'Encyclopaedia of Zionism'.

12. al-Misiri (1998: 57–67).
13. Professor at the American University in Cairo.
14. Amin (1998: 75–81).
15. al-Shaykh (1998: 96–9).
16. Sultan (1998b: 7–8).
17. al-Bishri (1998: 28–9).
18. Sultan (1998a: 5).
19. Ibid., pp. 4–5; Iskandar (1999: 96–106).
20. Sultan (1998b: 4–6).
21. Ibid., pp. 6–8.
22. As quoted from 'Imara (1998: 22).
23. Ibid., pp. 14–20.
24. Ibid., pp. 15–16; quoted from al-'Abda (1998: 30–32).
25. 'Imara (1998: 22).
26. As an example, al-Bishri names the traditional publication *Al-Hilal*, which was supported by the state from its founding in 1892. al-Bishri (1998: 23–5).
27. Ibid., p. 25.
28. Ibid., p. 26.
29. Ibid., pp. 26–7.
30. Ibid., p. 28.
31. Ibid., pp. 28–9; al-'Awwa 1998: 82–3).
32. al-'Azmeh (1992: 145–59).
33. al-Ghanushi (1998: 64).
34. Ibid., pp. 64–6.
35. Ibid., pp. 64–9.
36. Ibid., pp. 69–70.
37. Quoted from Habib (1998: 36–41); Hashim (1999: 79–89).
38. Habib (1998: 41–50); Madi (1998: 54–60).
39. Habib (1998: 50–3); 'Abd al-Majid (1999: 63–4).
40. Habib uses in this context the concept *fiqh al-darura* (the jurisprudence of necessity).
41. Habib (1999b: 25–30).
42. Ja'far (1998: 97–101).
43. Ibid., pp. 101–4.
44. In particular he mentions the non-violence initiative of the Egyptian *jama'a al-islamiyya* since July 1997.
45. Sultan (1999a: pp. 4–6); Sultan (1999b: 4–8).
46. Berger (1988: 101–62).
47. 'Restoring' here points to the affinity between contemporary critical thought in the Islamist spectrum and some premises of classical (Sunni) legal teaching. Also quoted from Jum'a (1999: 45–57).
48. On trends to westernization and secularization in modern religious discourse, see Schluchter (1991: 506–34).
49. al-Qaradawi (1998a: 6).
50. Ibid., pp. 7–14.
51. al-Qaradawi (1998b: 6–13); Jum'a (1999: 45–57).
52. Habib notes explicitly that the establishment of a state of the early Islamic type cannot be repeated.

53. Habib (1999b: 31–4).
54. al-Qaradawi (1998b: 70–4); Habib (1999a: 103–6).
55. In the view of the authors studied here this requires the establishment of democratic structures in the Islamist movements oriented on the *shura* principle.
56. It is noticeable that the terms civil society and citizens' society are used synonymously to refer to the intermediary spheres. Other authors reject civil society because of its western origin, and its use here indicates an open attitude to western concepts and systems of thought.
57. Habib (1998: 53–5); Habib (1999a: 103–6); Habib (1999b: 30–4); al-Ghanushi (1998: 70–4); Madi (2001: 60–2); Hashim (1999: 89–95).
58. Mahmud (2001).
59. as-Sayyid (2001); al-Misiri (2001).

References

al-'Abda, Muhammad. 'Nazarat fi masirat al-da'wa wa al-islah', *Al-Manar al-Jadid*, No. 1, Winter 1998, pp. 30–5.

Amin, Jalal. 'Tasghir al-kubara'', *Al-Manar al-Jadid*, No. 2, Spring 1998, pp. 75–81.

al-'Arabi, Shahrazad. 'Al-din wa al-dawla fi fikr jam'iyat al-'ulama' al-muslimin bi al-jaza'ir', in *Al-Manar al-Jadid*, No. 6, Spring 1999, pp. 35–41.

al-'Awwa, Muhammad Salim. 'Tajdid al-fiqh: fi al-mashru' al-hadari al-islami', *Al-Manar al-Jadid*, No. 2, Spring 1998, pp. 82–7.

al-'Azmeh, 'Aziz. *Al-'ilmaniyya min manzur mukhtalif* (Beirut: Markaz dirasat al-wihda al-'arabiyya, 1992).

Berger, Peter. *Zur Dialektik von Religion und Gesellschaft* (Frankfurt am Main: Fischer Taschenbuch Verlag, 1988).

al-Bishri, Tariq. 'Al-tajdid al-islami bayna qarn mada wa qarn yaji'', *Al-Manar al-Jadid*, No. 1, Winter 1998, pp. 23–9.

al-Ghanushi, Rashid. 'Hirat al-haraka al-islamiyya bayna al-dawla wa al-mujtama'', *Al-Manar al-Jadid*, No. 2, Spring 1998, pp. 64–74.

Habib, Kamal. 'Al-haraka al-islamiyya al-mu'asira: ru'ya min al-dakhil',*Al-Manar al-Jadid*, No. 1, Winter 1998, pp. 36–55.

—— 'Al-islamiyun wa al-siyasa wa al-mujtama' al-ahli', in *Al-Manar al-Jadid*, No. 5, 1999a, pp. 101–7.

—— 'Al-islamiyun wa al-intikhabat al-niyabiyya: ru'ya jadida', *Al-Manar al-Jadid*, No. 6, Spring 1999b, pp. 25–34.

Harb, Muhammad. 'Al-arbakaniyya: harakat Najm al-Din Arbakan', *Al-Manar al-Jadid*, No. 4, Autumn 1998, pp. 105–12.

Hashim, Muhammad. 'Al-sira' bayna al-haraka al-islamiyya wa al-sulta: al-asbab wa al-'ilaj', *Al-Manar al-Jadid*, No. 6, Spring 1999, pp. 79–95.

'Imara, Muhammad. 'Li-ma-za Al-Manar?', *Al-Manar al-Jadid*, No. 1, Winter 1998, pp. 11–22.

Iskandar, Amin. 'Jil al-wasat fi al-haraka al-wataniyya al-misriyya wa bina' jusur li al-mustaqbal', *Al-Manar al-Jadid*, No. 6, Spring 1999, pp. 96–106.

Ja'far, 'Ali. 'Ma-ba'd al-ahzab al-siyasiyya: qira'a fi tajrubat al-'amal al-islami ma'a al-siyasa', *Al-Manar al-Jadid*, No. 4, Autumn 1998, pp. 97–104.

Jum'a, 'Ali. 'Al-thabit wa al-mutaghayyir fi al-shari'a al-islamiyya', *Al-Manar al-Jadid*, No. 7, Summer 1999, pp. 45–57.

Abd al-Karim, Muhammad. 'Al-'aulama: 'alam thalith 'ala abwab qarn jadid', *Al-Manar al-Jadid*, No. 3, Summer 1998, pp. 32–45.

Khalifa, Muhammad. 'Al-haraka al-islamiyya al-turkiyya fi nisf qarn', *Al-Manar al-Jadid*, No. 2, Spring 1998, pp. 18–38.

Madi, Abu al-'ila. 'Jama'at al-'unf al-misriyya al-murtabita bi al-islam, al-judur al-tarikhiyya wa al-usul al-fikriyya wa al-mustaqbal', *Al-Manar al-Jadid*, No. 3, Summer 1998, pp.46–62.

Mahmud, Mustafa. 'Hal huwa intihar!' *Al-Ahram*, 3 November 2001.

'Abd al-Majid, Yusuf. 'Al-tayar al-asasi fi al-wataniyya al-misriyya bayna al-islamiyin wa al-qawmiyin wa al-libaraliyin', *Al-Manar al-Jadid*, No. 6, Spring 1999, pp. 62–74.

al-Misiri, Yusuf. 'Fashal al-namuzaj al-maddi fi tafsir zahirat al-insan', *Al-Manar al-Jadid*, No. 4, Autumn 1998, pp. 57–67.

—— 'Li-natafawad ma'an zalimin wa mazlumin', *Al-Hayat*, 11 October 2001.

al-Qaradawi, Yusuf. 'Fiqh al-waqi' wa taghayyur al-fatwa', *Al-Manar al-Jadid*, No. 3, Summer 1998a, pp. 6–15.

—— 'Fi fiqh al-taghyir', *Al-Manar al-Jadid*, No. 4, Autumn 1998b, pp. 6–13.

Rumih, Tal'at. 'Jil al-sab'inat, azmat nash'a am ma'ziq jil?', *Al-Manar al-Jadid*, No. 4, Autumn 1998, pp. 68–75.

Saqr, 'Abd al-'Aziz. 'Al-qawmiyya wa al-'ilmaniyya wa al-din: qira'a fi al-khibra al-gharbiyya', *Al-Manar al-Jadid*, No. 2, Spring 1998, pp. 39–48.

—— 'Al-din wa al-siyasa fi al-waqi' al-gharbi al-mu'asir', *Al-Manar al-Jadid*, No. 5, Winter 1999, pp. 48–64.

As-Sayyid, Ridwan. 'Isti'adat al-islam min man khatafuhu', *Al-Hayat*, 11 October 2001.

Schluchter, Wolfgang. 'Religion und Lebensführung'. Vol. 2. *Studien zu Max Webers Religions- und Herrschaftssoziologie* (Frankfurt am Main: Suhrkamp, 1991).

Sha'ban, Ahmad. 'Jil al-sab'inat fi al-siyasa al-misriyya', *Al-Manar al-Jadid*, No. 5, Winter 1999, pp. 76–85.

al-Sharif, Kamil. 'Al-shabab al-muslim wa al-'aulama', in *Al-Manar al-Jadid*, No. 7, Summer 1999, pp. 8–24.

al-Shaykh, Mamduh. 'Al-'amal al-ahli fi misr: al-darura wa al-mahzurat wa al-dularat', *Al-Manar al-Jadid*, No. 2, Spring 1998, pp. 96–9.

Sultan, Jamal. 'Hikayat Al-Manar al-Jadid', *Al-Manar al-Jadid*, No. 1, Winter 1998a, pp. 4–6.

—— 'Qimat al-hiwar', *Al-Manar al-Jadid*, No. 2, Spring 1998b, pp. 4–8.

—— 'Al-haraka al-islamiyya fi misr 'ala tariq al-jihad al-silmi', *Al-Manar al-Jadid*, No. 5, Winter 1999a, pp. 4–8.

—— 'Al-haraka al-islamiyya: humum wa amal', *Al-Manar al-Jadid*, No. 7, 1999b, pp. 4–7.

Tammam, Hussam. 'Manzur al-fikr al-islami fi tahlil al-'ilaqat al-dawliyya', *Al-Manar al-Jadid*, No. 1, Winter 1998, pp. 129–35.

About the Contributors

Frederick C. Abrahams was Senior Researcher at Human Rights Watch from 1995 to 2000, covering the South Balkans. He is co-author with Eric Stover and Gilles Peress of *A Village Destroyed: War Crimes in Kosovo,* published by University of California Press. He is currently writing a book on Albania's transition from communism.

Valérie Amiraux is a Research fellow at the Centre Universitaire de Recherches Administratives et Politiques de Picardie (CURAPP) and in the Centre National de la Recherche Scientifique (CNRS). Dr Amiraux is the author of *Acteurs de l'islam entre Allemagne et Turquie: appartenances religieuses et pratiques militantes* (Paris: L'Harmattan, 2001). Her main interests include political Islam, Islam in Europe, and the linkages between academic knowledge and policy-making.

John L. Esposito is University Professor and Professor of Religion and International Affairs at Georgetown University's Walsh School of Foreign Service. Founding Director of the Center for Muslim–Christian Understanding, Esposito is Editor-in-Chief of *The Oxford Encyclopedia of the Modern Islamic World* and *The Oxford History of Islam.* His other publications include *Unholy War: Terror in the Name of Islam; What Everyone Needs to Know about Islam; The Islamic Threat: Myth or Reality?; Islam: The Straight Path; Islam and Politics; Islam and Democracy* and *Makers of Contemporary Islam* (with John O. Voll); *Political Islam: Revolution, Radicalism, or Reform?; Iran at the Crossroads* (with R.K. Ramazani); *Islam and Secularism in the Middle East* (with Azzam Tamimi); *Islam, Gender and Social Change* (with Yvonne Haddad); and *Women in Muslim Family Law.*

Amr Hamzawy is a Research Fellow at the Centre for Middle Eastern Studies, Department of Political and Social Sciences, The Free University of Berlin, Germany. Dr Hamzawy is author of several articles in journals and periodicals in German, Arabic and English, and his research areas include Islamism, Contemporary Arab Intellectual Discourses, Civil Society and Democratization and Cultural Impacts of Globalization on Arab Countries.

Jan Hjärpe is a Professor of Islamology and History of Religions, at the Department of Theology and Religious studies, Lund University, Sweden. Professor Hjärpe is the author of 400 articles and essays and his books include *Politisk islam: Studier i muslimsk fundamentalism* [Political Islam: Studies in Islamic Fundamentalism] (1990), *Islams värld* [The World of Islam] (1993); *Islam och traditionen: religion i förändring* [Islam and Tradition: Religion and Change] (2002).

Azza Karam is a Programme Director at the World Conference on Religions for Peace (WCRP) in New York. She was Lecturer in Politics at Queen's University in Belfast, Northern Ireland, and also worked as a Senior Programme Officer at the International Institute for Democracy and Electoral Assistance (IDEA) in Stockholm, Sweden. Dr Karam has written several articles on political Islam, development, and conflict. Her books include *Women, Islamisms and the State* (1998 in English; 2000 in Arabic); and *Women in Parliament: Beyond Numbers* (1998).

Jan Nederveen Pieterse is a Professor at the University of Illinois at Urbana-Champaign, specializing in transnational sociology with focus on globalization, development studies and cultural analysis. Professor Nederveen Pieterse is the author of several books. He has taught in several countries, is co-editor of the *Review of International Political Economy* and advisory editor of several journals.

Index

Compiled by Sue Carlton